I ♥ Pumpkin

I ♥ Pumpkin

comforting recipes for cooking
with winter squash

RYLAND PETERS & SMALL
LONDON • NEW YORK

Designer: Paul Stradling
Editors: Alice Sambrook & Dawn Bates
Production: Mai-Ling Collyer
Art Director: Leslie Harrington
Editorial Director: Julia Charles
Publisher: Cindy Richards

Indexer: Hilary Bird

Published in 2018 by
Ryland Peters & Small
20–21 Jockey's Fields London
WC1R 4BW and
341 E 116th St
New York NY 10029

www.rylandpeters.com

Recipe collection compiled by Alice
Sambrook. Text © Acland Geddes, Belinda
Williams, Ben Fordham, Brian Glover,
Carol Hilker, Dunja Gulin, Elsa Peterson
Schepelern, Felipe Fuentes Cruz, Fiona
Beckett, Fiona Smith, Ghillie Basan, Hannah
Miles, Isidora Popovic, Jordan Bourke, Kathy
Kordalis, Laura Washburn, Leah Vanderveldt,
Maxine Clark, Nadia Arumugam, Ross
Dobson, Sarah Randall, Tori Haschka and
Ryland Peters & Small 2018

Design and photographs © Ryland Peters
& Small 2018

ISBN: 978-1-84975-971-7

A CIP record for this book is available from
the British Library.
US Library of Congress Cataloging-in-
Publication data has been applied for.

Printed and bound in China

notes

• Both British (Metric) and American (Imperial ounces plus US cups) are included in these recipes for your convenience; however, it is important to work with one set of measurements only and not alternate between the two within a recipe.

• All spoon measurements are level unless otherwise specified.

• All eggs are medium (UK) or large (US), unless specified as large, in which case US extra-large should be used. Uncooked or partially cooked eggs should not be served to the very old, frail, young children, pregnant women or those with compromised immune systems.

• Ovens should be preheated to the specified temperatures. We recommend using an oven thermometer. If using a fan-assisted oven, adjust temperatures according to the manufacturer's instructions.

• When a recipe calls for the grated zest of citrus fruit, buy unwaxed fruit and wash well before using. If you can only find treated fruit, scrub well in warm soapy water before using.

contents

introduction

There are myriad varieties of squash, from delicate summer squash, such as courgettes/zucchini, to hardy winter squash, including pumpkins. It's the latter that you'll find in this collection of over 60 cozy and comforting recipes.

Winter squash can take robust treatment when cooking. Roasting or pan-frying concentrates its flavour to a sweet, chestnutty richness. It makes a great base for soups and stews, but is also wonderful stirred into pasta or rice dishes, or layered and baked in creamy gratins. As you'll discover, it has a real affinity with a wide range of ingredients: its nutty sweetness works well with salty tastes such as goat's cheese and it can be beautifully seasoned with musky sage, cumin or nutmeg, or the spicy heat of chilli/chile. Mostly, we think of savoury flavours when we cook with squash, but it picks up the sweetness of sugar too. Used in pies, tarts, puddings and preserves, it cries out for warm spices such as cinnamon and ginger as well as a hint of citrus sharpness and the smooth richness of butter and cream.

Butternut is undoubtedly the most popular winter squash and no wonder. It tastes deliciously sweet and nutty when roasted or pan-fried and it isn't as dry-fleshed or starchy as some varieties. You can use it for almost all the savoury recipes in this book, but there is a wealth of other varieties, so do shop around and experiment. For many of the sweet recipes in this book, store-bought pumpkin purée is used, but if you can't find it there are instructions on how to make your own.

One of the few varieties of winter squash that isn't that good to eat is probably the most familiar – the red-orange Halloween or Cinderella pumpkin. It's really an ornamental pumpkin and the flesh tends to be fibrous and watery. You can use it to make a base for puréed soups, but it's really best kept for lantern making!

From snacks and salads to pasta, pies and other sweet treats, the recipes that follow are designed to help you discover the many savoury and sweet delights of cooking with this wonderfully versatile ingredient. Enjoy!

snacks & light bites

spiced squash & feta filo pastries

The sweet taste of pan-fried or roasted squash works particularly well with the salty taste of fresh feta cheese. Add a bite of chilli/chile and a crisp wrapping of buttery filo pastry and you have the ideal party nibble to serve with drinks or a delicious treat for picnics.

3 tablespoons olive oil

¼ teaspoon dried chilli/hot red pepper flakes

400 g/3⅓ cups prepared squash, such as butternut, diced

6 spring onions/scallions, thinly sliced

1 rounded teaspoon cumin seeds, lightly crushed

1 garlic clove, finely chopped

2 tablespoons each finely chopped flat-leaf parsley and dill

200 g/7 oz. feta cheese, diced

freshly squeezed lemon juice, to taste

8 sheets of filo/phyllo pastry, thawed if frozen

100 g/7 tablespoons unsalted butter, melted

2 tablespoons sesame seeds

sea salt and freshly ground black pepper

MAKES 24 SMALL PASTRIES

Make the filling first. Heat the oil in a large frying pan/skillet over medium heat. Add the chilli/hot red pepper flakes and squash and fry gently, stirring every now and then, until the squash is tender and lightly browned, about 7–8 minutes. Add the spring onions/scallions, cumin and garlic, then fry gently for another 2–3 minutes. Allow to cool, then mix in a bowl with the herbs and feta. Season to taste with lemon juice, salt and pepper.

Preheat the oven to 190°C (375°F) Gas 5. Lightly grease one or two baking sheets. Working with one sheet of filo/phyllo at a time (and keeping the remainder covered to prevent it drying out), cut each sheet lengthways into three strips.

Brush each strip with a little melted butter. Put a heaped tablespoon of filling at one end of each strip, then fold up the pastry to enclose the filling in a triangle. Continue to fold up the strip of pastry to make a multi-layered triangle. Place each triangle on a prepared baking sheet as you finish it and continue until all the filo/phyllo and filling has been used.

Brush the top of each pastry with a little melted butter, sprinkle with a few sesame seeds, then bake in the preheated oven for 20–25 minutes until crisp and golden brown.

roasted flat mushrooms

WITH SPICED SQUASH & CHICKPEA STUFFING

1 small squash (about 900 g/
7½ cups), peeled, deseeded
and diced

5–6 tablespoons olive oil

a small bunch of thyme,
chopped

¼ teaspoon dried chilli/hot red
pepper flakes

1 garlic clove, chopped

1 x 400-g/14-oz. can chickpeas,
drained

½–1 teaspoon ground toasted
cumin seeds

freshly squeezed lemon juice,
to taste

1–2 tablespoons chopped
flat-leaf parsley

1–2 tablespoons crème fraîche
or sour cream (optional)

8 large, flat portobello
mushrooms, stalks removed

4 tablespoons toasted
pumpkin seeds

sea salt and freshly ground
black pepper

for the sauce

1 garlic clove

a pinch of coarse sea salt

3–4 tablespoons tahini

freshly squeezed lemon juice

4–5 tablespoons plain yogurt

1 tablespoon chopped mint

SERVES 4

This is a delicious starter, but also good enough to
serve as a meat-free main with salad if you're looking
for a light lunch.

Preheat the oven to 220°C (425°F) Gas 7. Toss the squash with
3 tablespoons of the oil, 1 teaspoon thyme, the chilli/hot red pepper
flakes and garlic. Season and put on a baking sheet. Cover with foil
and cook in the preheated oven for about 30 minutes until tender,
then uncover and cook for a further 10 minutes. Let cool and put in
a food processor with the chickpeas. Whizz to make a rough purée.
Season to taste with salt, pepper, cumin and lemon juice, then stir
in the parsley. If the purée is very dry, add the crème fraîche or sour
cream, if using, or a little water.

Meanwhile, put the mushrooms, gill-side uppermost, on an oiled
baking sheet. Season and sprinkle with a few thyme leaves. Drizzle
with the remaining oil and a good squeeze of lemon juice. Roast,
uncovered, in the preheated oven for 15 minutes until just cooked.
Remove from the oven and reduce the heat to 190°C (375°F) Gas 5.

Distribute the stuffing between the mushrooms. Scatter with the
pumpkin seeds and a few thyme sprigs. Spoon over a little of
the mushroom cooking juices, then return them to the oven for
10 minutes to heat through.

To make the sauce, mash the garlic with the salt in a bowl, then
gradually work in 3 tablespoons tahini, followed by 1 tablespoon
lemon juice. When smooth, gradually work in the yogurt, then taste
and add more lemon juice and/or tahini as necessary. Stir in the
mint and serve with the mushrooms.

squash, goat's cheese & tomato tarts

WITH PARMESAN PASTRY

for the pastry

180 g/1⅓ cups plain/
all-purpose flour

90 g/6 tablespoons unsalted
butter, chilled

a pinch each of salt and
cayenne pepper

80 g/2¾ oz. Parmesan cheese,
freshly grated

1 medium egg yolk

for the filling

3 tablespoons olive oil

1 large onion, thinly sliced

350 g/3 cups squash, diced

2 teaspoons chopped
thyme leaves

150 g/5 oz. goat's cheese,
crumbled

100 g/3½ oz. sun-dried
tomatoes in oil, drained and
roughly chopped

200 ml/¾ cup double/heavy
cream

2 large/extra large eggs

2 tablespoons snipped chives

sea salt and freshly ground
black pepper

6 individual, 9-cm/3½-in., fluted,
loose-bottomed metal tart pans

SERVES 6

These flavoursome tarts bring together delicious ingredients that work so well with the sweet, dense flesh of winter squash—sharp goat's cheese, salty Parmesan, caramelly sun-dried tomatoes and onion. They are best served just warm, rather than piping hot.

To make the pastry, put the flour, butter, salt and cayenne pepper in a food processor and whizz until the mixture resembles breadcrumbs. Add the Parmesan, egg yolk and 1½ tablespoons iced water and whizz again until it forms a dough. Shape the pastry dough into a smooth ball on a work surface, wrap in foil and chill in the refrigerator for at least 40 minutes.

Preheat the oven to 190°C (375°F) Gas 5. Roll out the chilled pastry thinly and line 6 individual tart pans. Protect the sides with strips of foil, then chill for a further 30 minutes. Transfer to a baking sheet and cook in the preheated oven for 12 minutes. Remove the foil and return them to the oven to cook for another 5–6 minutes until pale brown.

To make the filling, heat the oil in a frying pan/skillet and add the onion and a pinch of salt. Cover, reduce the heat to low and cook, stirring once or twice, for 10–12 minutes until softened but not browned. Add the squash and cook over medium heat, uncovered and stirring occasionally, until the squash is tender and lightly browned. Add the thyme, stir a few minutes more, then take off the heat and let cool.

Arrange the squash, cheese and tomatoes in the part-baked tart cases. Beat together the cream and eggs, add the chives and season with salt and pepper. Carefully pour the mixture into the cases, return them to the hot oven and cook for 25–30 minutes until the custard is set and puffed up. Let cool slightly before serving.

squash & sage frittata

There is something about the musty sharpness of sage that works so well with the sweetness of caramelized squash. This frittata is very adaptable – cut into wedges and serve with a peppery green salad for a great lunch or cut into bite-sized pieces and serve as a nibble with drinks.

4 tablespoons olive oil

2 large sweet onions, halved and thinly sliced

¼ teaspoon dried chilli/hot red pepper flakes (or more to taste), crushed

2 garlic cloves, peeled and halved

1 butternut squash (about 650 g/5 cups), peeled, deseeded and diced

1 tablespoon finely shredded sage leaves

8 large/extra large eggs

2–3 tablespoons chopped flat-leaf parsley

15 g/1 tablespoon butter

150 g/5 oz. firm goat's cheese, cubed

sea salt and freshly ground black pepper

SERVES 4 OR CUTS INTO 24–30 PIECES FOR AN APPETIZER

In a medium-large frying pan/skillet with a lid, heat the oil over medium heat. Add the onions and 2 good pinches of salt. Stir, then cover and reduce the heat to low. Cook very gently, stirring occasionally, until the onions are meltingly soft and golden yellow, about 20 minutes.

Raise the heat slightly and add the hot red pepper/chilli flakes, garlic and squash. Stir to cover in the oily onions and cook gently, stirring frequently, until the squash is just tender, about 10 minutes. Discard the garlic. Fry the squash a little more until it starts to brown, then stir in the sage and cook for a few more minutes. Let it cool slightly.

In a bowl, whisk the eggs and beat in the parsley, then stir in the cooked squash and onions. Season with a little salt and black pepper. Put the frying pan/skillet back over medium heat and preheat the grill/broiler to medium. Add the butter to the pan, and as it foams, pour in the egg and squash mixture and use a spatula to level it. Scatter the goat's cheese evenly over the top. Cook for about 5–6 minutes until the underside is golden brown and set.

Put the frittata under the preheated grill/broiler and cook until it is evenly browned, slightly puffed up and the egg is fully set. Serve warm or at room temperature.

roasted pumpkin wedges

WITH LIME & SPICES

This is a great way to enjoy pumpkin. Serve these spicy wedges on their own or with any grilled, roasted or barbecued meat or poultry dish. Save the seeds and roast them lightly with a little oil and coarse salt as a nibble.

1 medium-sized pumpkin, halved lengthways, deseeded, and cut into 6–8 segments

2 teaspoons coriander seeds

1 teaspoon cumin seeds

1 teaspoon fennel seeds

1–2 teaspoons ground cinnamon

2 dried red chillies/chiles, chopped

2 garlic cloves

2 tablespoons olive oil

coarse sea salt

finely grated zest of 1 lime

6 wooden or metal skewers, for serving (optional)

SERVES 6

Preheat the oven to 200°C (400°F) Gas 6.

Using a mortar and pestle, grind all the dried spices with the salt.

Add the garlic and a little of the olive oil to form a paste. Rub the mixture over the pumpkin wedges and place them, skin-side down, in a baking dish. Cook them in the preheated oven for 35–40 minutes, or until tender. Sprinkle over the lime zest and serve hot, threaded onto skewers, if using.

pumpkin fondue

1 large red or orange pumpkin, about 25–30 cm/10–12 in. diameter, or 4 small, round red onion squash or similar

3–4 tablespoons olive oil

a few torn thyme sprigs or sage leaves

sea salt and freshly ground black pepper

for the fondue

2 teaspoons potato flour or cornflour/cornstarch

300 ml/10 fl. oz. dry white wine, such as Riesling or Grüner Veltliner, or dry cider

1 garlic clove, peeled and halved

1 bay leaf

400 g/14 oz. Gruyère, derinded and thinly sliced or grated/shredded

2 tablespoons Kirsch (optional)

250–300 g/9–10½ oz. Taleggio or Fontina cheese, derinded and thinly sliced or grated

4 tablespoons crème fraîche or sour cream

SERVES 4

Serving fondue in a baked pumpkin shell is not just about fun presentation – the sweet, tender squash is wonderful with the salty, sharp richness of the cheese. Use a whole, large pumpkin for everyone to dip into or small individual squashes. Serve with cubes of crusty bread for dipping and spoons for scraping the baked squash from the shell.

Preheat the oven to 190°C (375°F) Gas 5. Cut a lid off the pumpkin or the squashes and, if necessary, take a thin slice off the base so that the shell(s) will stand upright without wobbling.

Scoop out the seeds and enough flesh to leave a shell about 2.5 cm/1 in. thick (red onion squash are fine as they are, just remove the seeds). Rub with the oil inside and out, season with salt and pepper, add a few herb sprigs to the cavity and bake in the preheated oven for about 50 minutes for a large pumpkin or 40 minutes for small squash. Bake the lids as well, if liked, for around 20–25 minutes, depending on size.

Meanwhile, make the cheese fondue. Mix the potato flour with 2–3 tablespoons of the wine and set aside. Put the remaining wine in a medium-sized, heavy-based saucepan over medium heat and bring to the boil. Simmer for 2–3 minutes, then add the garlic and bay leaf and reduce the heat. Add the Gruyère cheese and, stirring all the time, allow it to melt. When melted, remove and discard the garlic and bay leaf, then stir in the potato flour mixture and the Kirsch (if using) until smooth. Add the Taleggio and stir frequently over low heat until the cheese melts. Add the cream, season to taste and stir until you have a smooth, velvety texture.

To serve, pour the fondue into the baked shell(s), cover with the lid(s), if using, and carry to the table.

prosciutto & pumpkin terrine

WITH CELERIAC SALAD

150 g/5 oz. thin slices prosciutto

750 g/6¼ cups pumpkin

2 tablespoons olive oil

2 tablespoons fresh thyme leaves, plus sprigs to garnish

3 eggs

1 tablespoon maple syrup

¼ teaspoon ground nutmeg

½ teaspoon sea salt

¼ teaspoon freshly ground black pepper

for the celeriac salad

1 celeriac

3 tablespoons chopped fresh flat-leaf parsley

2 tablespoons good-quality mayonnaise

1 tablespoon freshly squeezed lemon juice

1 tablespoon olive oil

sea salt and freshly ground black pepper

a 25-cm|10-in. narrow loaf pan, lightly oiled

SERVES 8–10

This light, tasty terrine is fantastic for summer lunches, and perfect to snack on. It is best served just warm or at room temperature – if it is too hot, it will be hard to slice. Try to cut between the prosciutto slices.

Preheat the oven to 180°C (350°F) Gas 4.

Cut the prosciutto into 2-cm/¾-in. strips and lay them across the width of the prepared loaf pan.

Cut the skin off the pumpkin and discard it. Cut the flesh into 3-cm/1¼-in. cubes and toss with the olive oil and the thyme leaves. Spread in a roasting dish and roast in the oven for 30 minutes until soft.

Leave the pumpkin to cool slightly, then put in a food processor and process to a purée. Add the eggs, maple syrup, nutmeg, salt and pepper and process until well mixed. Pour the mixture into the loaf pan and bake in the oven for 30 minutes. Cover the terrine with a sheet of oiled foil and bake for a further 15 minutes until the pumpkin is set. Remove from the oven and leave to cool for at least 15 minutes before serving. Turn the terrine out, then invert so that the prosciutto is around the sides and base.

To make the celeriac salad, finely grate the celeriac into a bowl using a mandoline or grater. Toss with the remaining ingredients. Serve the terrine warm or at room temperature, garnished with thyme sprigs, with the celeriac salad.

squash, blue cheese & sage pizza

Sweet-tasting squash and tangy blue cheese is a winning combination in this delicious pizza that will delight your vegetarian friends and family.

for the pizza dough

6 g/1 teaspoon dried yeast

700 g/5 cups strong bread flour

2 pinches of sea salt

70 ml/scant ⅓ cup extra virgin olive oil

semolina, for dusting

pizza sheet or large baking sheet

pizza stone or large heavy baking sheet

MAKES 8 PIZZAS

topping (for 1 pizza)

100 g/1 scant cup butternut squash, sliced and roasted

60 g/½ cup blue cheese, crumbled

50 g/⅓ cup mozzarella, torn

approx. 10 sage leaves (depending on size)

olive oil, to drizzle

sea salt and freshly ground black pepper

Prepare the dough – combine the yeast and 100 ml/scant ½ cup lukewarm water in a bowl, stir to dissolve and set aside until foamy (approx. 5 minutes). Combine the flour, salt and olive oil in an electric mixer fitted with a dough hook. Add the yeast mixture and 320 ml/scant 1½ cups water and knead until well combined. Knead on a low speed in the mixer for approx. 5 minutes until a smooth, elastic dough is formed. Let the dough stand at room temperature, covered with a damp kitchen towel, until doubled in size (1 hour) or refrigerate overnight to prove – this can be done the night before and brought to room temperature (approx. 2 hours) before you bake.

Turn out the dough onto a flour-dusted surface and knock back/punch down, then bring the mixture just together to form a smooth, soft dough. Do not overwork. Divide the dough into 8 balls, then place on a lightly floured surface and cover with a lightly floured kitchen towel until doubled in size (20 minutes).

Working with one ball of dough at a time, place onto a semolina-dusted 22-cm/8½-in. pizza sheet and press outward from the centre to flatten, making the edges slightly thicker than the centre (if you don't have a pizza sheet, use a baking sheet dusted with semolina).

Put a pizza stone or a large, heavy baking sheet upside down on the top shelf of the oven. Preheat the oven to 220°C (425°F) Gas 7 for at least 30 minutes.

Scatter a dough base with the butternut squash, both cheeses, and sage leaves, then drizzle with olive oil and season. Transfer to the hot pizza stone or baking sheet and bake for 8–10 minutes until crisp. Serve hot with a little more olive oil.

Repeat with the remaining bases (or try different toppings).

roasted butternut squash grilled cheese sandwich WITH SAGE BUTTER

This roasted squash sandwich has a hidden twist thanks to the sage-infused brown butter. Using excellent Parmesan cheese is the key, so don't scrimp!

250 g/2 cups butternut squash pieces, fresh or frozen

salt and freshly ground black pepper

4 slices white or sourdough bread

unsalted butter, softened

4 tablespoons ricotta

2 thin slices mild cheese, such as Gouda or Fontina

1 tablespoon vegetable oil

2–3 tablespoons grated/shredded Parmesan

for the sage butter

50 g/3 tablespoons unsalted butter

a few sprigs fresh sage, leaves stripped

squeeze of fresh lemon juice

SERVES 2

Preheat the oven to 200°C (400°F) Gas 6. Coat the butternut squash with the oil and arrange in a single layer on a baking sheet. Season and roast until tender and golden brown, around 20–30 minutes. Remove from the oven and crush coarsely. Set aside.

For the sage butter, melt the butter in a small saucepan until gently sizzling and beginning to deepen in colour. Add the sage leaves and remove from the heat as soon as the leaves crisp up. Add the lemon juice and let stand until needed.

Spread softened butter on the outside of the bread slices on one side and spread two of the slices on the non-buttered side with the ricotta, evenly divided.

Put two slices of bread in the pan/skillet, butter-side down. If you can only fit one slice in your pan/skillet, you'll need to cook one sandwich at a time. Top each of the bread slices with one slice of Gouda or Fontina and some of the crushed butternut squash, spread evenly to the edges. Drizzle over liberal amounts of the sage butter, but no more than half per slice. Sprinkle half of the Parmesan over each slice and cover with the remaining bread slices, ricotta side down.

Turn the heat to medium and cook the first side for 3–5 minutes until deep golden, pressing gently with a spatula. Carefully turn with a spatula and cook on the second side, for 2–3 minutes more or until deep golden brown all over.

Remove from the pan/skillet, transfer to a plate and cut in half diagonally. Let cool for a few minutes before serving. Repeat for the remaining sandwich if necessary. Any remaining sage butter can be drizzled over the sandwiches before serving.

salads & sides

spiced pumpkin & spelt salad

WITH GOAT'S CHEESE

Spelt is one of the most ancient cultivated wheats – rich in vitamins and minerals and in a readily digestible form, unlike ordinary wheat. Because of its high nutritional value, it has recently become a more popular choice. If you can't find pumpkin, substitute with butternut squash.

50 g/⅓ cup whole spelt

400 g/3⅓ cups peeled and deseeded pumpkin flesh

65 ml/¼ cup olive oil

½ teaspoon sea salt

½ teaspoon Spanish smoked sweet paprika (pimentón dulce)

¼ teaspoon dried chilli/hot red pepper flakes

¼ teaspoon ground allspice

50 g/⅓ cup unsalted cashew nuts

1 tablespoon white wine vinegar

100 g/4 oz. soft goat's cheese

4 handfuls of wild rocket/arugula

freshly ground black pepper

a baking sheet lined with baking paper

SERVES 4

Put the spelt in a large saucepan with plenty of boiling water. Set over high heat, bring back to the boil and cook for about 30 minutes, until just tender yet still firm to the bite. Drain well and set aside.

Preheat the oven to 180°C (350°F) Gas 4.

Cut the pumpkin flesh into large bite-sized chunks and put in a bowl with half of the oil, salt, paprika, chilli/hot red pepper flakes and allspice. Toss to coat the pumpkin in the spiced oil. Tumble the pumpkin onto the prepared baking sheet and pour over any spiced oil from the bowl. Cook in the preheated oven for about 20 minutes.

Remove from the oven, scatter over the cashews and return to the oven for 8–10 minutes more, until the cashews are golden and the pumpkin tender. Remove from the oven and set aside.

Combine the remaining oil and vinegar in a small bowl.

Put the spelt, spiced pumpkin, cashews, goat's cheese and rocket/arugula in a large bowl and gently toss to combine, being careful not to break up the cheese or pumpkin too much. Pour over the dressing and season well with black pepper. Serve immediately.

pearl barley & roast pumpkin salad

WITH GREEN BEANS

Pearl barley is a great addition to salads as it manages to retain a bit of texture and is one of the rare white ingredients – this makes it very useful for improving the look of your salads. When it comes to green beans in salads, keep them whole and cook them correctly, making sure they retain that satisfying crunch when you bite into them.

500 g/4 cups pumpkin, peeled and cut into 3-cm/1¼-in. cubes

200 g/generous 1 cup pearl barley

olive oil, for roasting

400 g/14 oz. green beans, topped but not tailed

100 g/3½ oz. sundried tomatoes, roughly chopped

20 pitted black olives

1 tablespoon capers

1 red onion, sliced

1 bunch fresh basil, roughly chopped

1 garlic clove, crushed

sea salt and freshly ground black pepper

SERVES 4–6

Preheat the oven to 200°C (400°F) Gas 6.

Toss the pumpkin with a little olive oil and sea salt in a roasting pan. Roast for 20–25 minutes, until soft but not disintegrating.

In the meantime, bring a pan of salted water to the boil and cook the pearl barley for 20–30 minutes. It's impossible to give a precise cooking time, as each batch seems to be different (the same seems to apply to dried chickpeas, for some reason). You want the grains to be al dente, but not chalky or overly chewy. When they're ready, drain them and set aside.

For the beans, bring another pan of salted water to the boil and prepare a bowl of iced water. Add the beans and cook for 3–5 minutes. Test them by giving them a bend; you want them to be flexible, but still have a nice snap if you push them too far. Once cooked, drain them and drop them immediately into the iced water. This 'refreshing' process will halt the cooking process and help keep the beans perfectly cooked and vibrantly green.

To assemble the salad, mix the pearl barley with the sundried tomatoes, olives, capers, red onion, basil and garlic. Add this to the roast pumpkin and green beans and stir gently until well combined. Drizzle with a little olive oil and serve.

Tagine of spicy roasted pumpkin wedges
WITH LIME

This is a tasty way of enjoying pumpkin. These spicy wedges can be served as an accompaniment to other tagines, or on their own with spicy couscous and a salad. Save the seeds and roast them lightly with a little oil and coarse salt to serve as a quick snack.

1 small or ½ medium-sized pumpkin

2 teaspoons coriander seeds

1 teaspoon cumin seeds

1 teaspoon fennel seeds

1–2 teaspoons ground cinnamon

2 dried red chillies/chiles, finely chopped

1 teaspoon sea salt

2 garlic cloves, crushed

2–3 tablespoons olive or pumpkin seed oil

1–2 tablespoons honey

1–2 limes, cut into wedges, to serve

SERVES 4–6

Preheat the oven to 200°C (400°F) Gas 6.

Cut the pumpkin in half lengthways and scoop out the seeds with a spoon. Slice each pumpkin half into 4–6 thin wedges, like crescent moons, and arrange them, skin-side down, in a circle in the base of a wide tagine or in a heavy-based casserole.

Using a mortar and pestle, grind all the dried spices with the salt. Add the garlic and enough oil to form a paste. Rub the spicy paste over the pumpkin wedges and drizzle the rest of the oil over them.

Pop the tagine in the preheated oven and roast the pumpkin wedges for 35–40 minutes, until tender. Drizzle the honey over the wedges and return to the oven for a further 10 minutes. Sprinkle a little salt over the pumpkin wedges and serve hot with the lime to squeeze over them.

roasted pumpkin

WITH CHARD & MUSHROOMS

This warming dish has a satisfying, spicy kick. Served alongside mushrooms and chard, it is a delicious meal in its own right or makes a flavoursome side dish that will enhance any meal.

½ medium 1–1.5 kg/2–3 lb. pumpkin

4 tablespoons olive oil

a pinch of dried oregano

½ teaspoon ground cumin

2 dried Guajillo chillies/chiles, seeded and stalks removed

200 g/6½ oz. Swiss chard (or spinach)

200 g/6½ oz. wild mushrooms

½ red onion

2 garlic cloves

50 g/⅓ cup shelled pumpkin seeds

sea salt and ground black pepper

SERVES 4

Preheat the oven to 180°C (350°F) Gas 4.

Leave the seeds in the pumpkin, then cut it into 4 wedges and arrange in a roasting dish.

Put 2 tablespoons of the olive oil in a bowl and mix in ½ teaspoon salt, ½ teaspoon pepper, the oregano and cumin. Brush the mixture over the pumpkin wedges. Roast the pumpkin in the preheated oven for 30–35 minutes. When it is ready, you should be able to slide a sharp knife easily into the flesh.

While the pumpkin is cooking, put the chillies/chiles and 250 ml/1 cup water in a saucepan, bring to the boil, then cook for 5 minutes. Transfer the cooked chillies/chiles and their water to a food processor and whizz for 2–3 minutes, then set aside.

Clean the chard, cut off and discard the stems and roughly chop the leaves. Roughly chop the wild mushrooms, onion and garlic.

Put the pumpkin seeds in a dry frying pan/skillet over low heat. Stir continuously for 10 minutes, taking care not to let them burn.

Heat the remaining oil in a large saucepan, then fry the mushrooms, onion and garlic over high heat for 1 minute. Add the chard and fry for 2–3 minutes. Add the puréed chillies/chiles and a pinch of salt and pepper and cook for 5 minutes. Remove from the heat, add the pumpkin seeds and mix everything well.

Serve each pumpkin wedge with a portion of vegetables beside it. Eat as it is, or with warm bread.

stuffed sugar pumpkins

WITH PESTO & GOAT'S CHEESE

Choose small sugar pumpkins or butternut squash for this recipe (or just use the bottom half and keep the top piece for other recipes). Serve with salad for a main-course vegetarian lunch or as a tasty side dish.

4 small sugar pumpkins or butternut squash, washed and dried

2 small red onions, diced

16–20 cherry tomatoes, halved

a large handful of basil leaves

4 tablespoons pesto

2 small goat's cheeses or mozzarella, torn into pieces

olive oil, for drizzling

sea salt and freshly ground black pepper

SERVES 4

Preheat the oven to 200°C (400°F) Gas 6.

If the butternuts are small, halve them lengthways and scoop out the seeds. If large, cut them off just as they start to narrow into a waist – you're aiming for a hollow receptacle. If using sugar pumpkins, cut off a 'lid' and reserve. Scoop out with an ice-cream scoop to make smooth.

Put the onions in a sieve/strainer set over a bowl and cover with boiling water. Leave for about 2 minutes, then drain, pat dry with kitchen paper and distribute among the pumpkins. Add the tomato halves, the basil leaves, a generous tablespoon or two of pesto, then the goat's cheeses or mozzarella. Sprinkle with sea salt and freshly ground black pepper. Each of the hollows should be nicely filled with the ingredients.

Brush the pumpkins all over with olive oil, brushing the top of the cheese. Set the 'lids', if any, slightly askew. Arrange in an oiled roasting pan or dish and cook in the preheated oven until tender. Test with a metal skewer after 20 minutes, then again every 5–10 minutes until done (the time will depend on the size of your pumpkins).

Serve with a crisp, peppery salad.

pumpkin & rice gratin

Unlike a conventional gratin, this version has rice, which gives it a more interesting texture and makes it substantial enough to be a meal on its own, served with a green salad.

1.5 kg/12½ cups pumpkin, peeled, deseeded and cut into small cubes

3 tablespoons olive oil

100 g/½ cup long grain rice

a sprig of thyme

3 tablespoons fresh breadcrumbs

a small handful of flat-leaf parsley, finely chopped

3 tablespoons crème fraîche or sour cream

75 g/2½ oz. Gruyère cheese, finely grated

coarse sea salt and freshly ground black pepper

a large baking dish, greased with butter

SERVES 6

Put the pumpkin cubes in a large saucepan with 2 tablespoons of the oil, a pinch of salt and 250 ml/1 cup water. Cook over a low heat for 20–30 minutes, stirring often, until soft and adding more water as necessary.

Meanwhile, put the rice and the remaining 1 tablespoon oil in a separate saucepan and cook over medium heat, stirring to coat the grains. Add 250 ml/1 cup water, the thyme and a pinch of salt and bring to the boil. Cover and simmer for 10 minutes, until almost tender. Drain and discard the thyme.

Preheat the oven to 200°C (400°F) Gas 6. Mix the breadcrumbs with the parsley and a pinch of salt. Set aside.

Mash the cooked pumpkin into a coarse purée with a wooden spoon and stir in the cooked rice and crème fraîche or sour cream. Taste – the topping and cheese will add flavour, but the pumpkin mixture should be seasoned as well.

Spoon the pumpkin mixture into the prepared baking dish, spreading evenly. Sprinkle the cheese over the top, then follow with the breadcrumbs. Bake in the preheated oven for 20–30 minutes, until browned. Serve hot.

roast pumpkin & garlic polenta

Roast pumpkin and roast garlic are cleverly used here for a lighter polenta/cornmeal that is still full of flavour, but that doesn't require lavish amounts of butter and cheese.

1 medium pumpkin or 1 large butternut squash

5 large garlic cloves, unpeeled

3 tablespoons sunflower or grapeseed oil

40 g/3 tablespoons butter

50 g/1¾ oz. Parmesan cheese, grated, plus extra to taste

1.2 litres/5 cups vegetable stock, plus a little extra as necessary

250 g/generous 2 cups good-quality Italian polenta/cornmeal

sea salt and freshly ground black pepper

a large roasting pan

SERVES 6

Preheat the oven to 190°C (375°F) Gas 5.

Halve the pumpkin. Cut one half into quarters and scoop out the seeds. Quarter the other half, scoop out the seeds, cut each quarter into 2 or 3 pieces and cut away the skin with a sharp knife. Put all the pumpkin in a roasting pan along with the garlic cloves. Drizzle with the oil, mix well together and season generously with salt and pepper. Roast in the preheated oven for about 35–40 minutes until soft.

Remove the quartered pumpkin from the pan and set the rest aside to be reheated just before serving. Scrape the flesh off the skin and place in a food processor. Pop the roasted garlic cloves out of their skins and add to the pumpkin and whizz until smooth. Add the butter and Parmesan, whizz again and season.

Cook the polenta/cornmeal in the vegetable stock, following the instructions on the packet, taking care to whisk well to avoid lumps. Add the pumpkin and garlic purée to the cooked polenta/cornmeal and mix well. Add a little extra stock if needed to give a slightly sloppy consistency. Check the seasoning, adding more salt, pepper and Parmesan to taste. Reheat the pumpkin pieces briefly in a microwave or frying pan/skillet and serve on top of the polenta/cornmeal.

thanksgiving roast pumpkin

STUFFED WITH SWEET POTATO MASH & MARSHMALLOWS

If you're looking for a sweet side dish, try this unique Thanksgiving roast pumpkin dish topped with marshmallows and honey. It's simply delicious – and it may mean you don't crave that dessert after!

1 small pumpkin, about 15 cm/ 6 in. across

olive oil, for roasting

4 large sweet potatoes, cut into equal chunks

1 cinnamon stick

2 cloves

50 g/3½ tablespoons butter

75 ml/scant ⅓ cup double/ heavy cream

1 teaspoon ground cinnamon

¼ teaspoon ground nutmeg

¼ teaspoon ground ginger

1 teaspoon caster/superfine sugar

1 teaspoon clear honey, plus extra for drizzling

30 g/1 oz. pecans

30 g/1 oz. mini marshmallows

sea salt, to taste

SERVES 4 AS A SIDE FOR A ROAST DINNER

Preheat the oven to 220°C (425°F) Gas 7.

Cut the top off the pumpkin and discard it. Using a sturdy spoon, scoop out all the seeds and pith from the centre and discard them. Drizzle a little olive oil and salt into the pumpkin and roast for around 40 minutes, or until it is lightly browned at the edges and the inside is cooked through. Be careful when you open the oven, as you'll get a faceful of scalding steam. Once cooked, remove and set aside.

While the pumpkin is cooking, put the sweet potatoes in a pan and cover with tepid water. Add the cloves, cinnamon sticks and a pinch of salt. Bring to the boil and cook, uncovered, for about 30 minutes, until a knife passes through them with little or no resistance. Drain in a colander, remove the cinnamon stick and cloves and return to the pan. Add the butter, cream, sugar, ground cinnamon, nutmeg and ginger. Mash with a potato masher. It won't be easy to get a totally smooth consistency, but do your best. Add the honey and season with salt to taste.

Spoon the sweet potato mash into the hollowed-out pumpkin and top with the pecans, mini marshmallows and a little drizzle of honey. The residual heat of the mash should be enough to melt the marshmallows, but you can always pop it in the oven for 5 more minutes if necessary.

soups

pumpkin & mushroom soup

This deliciously rich soup is a wonderful, vibrant gold colour. The silky nature of the cep mushrooms works really well with the smoothness of the soup and the addition of truffle oil, used at your discretion, elevates it from the everyday to something really special.

50 g/3½ tablespoons butter

2 white onions, diced

2 garlic cloves, finely chopped

1 small pumpkin, peeled, deseeded and diced

½ butternut squash, peeled, deseeded and diced

1.5 litres/6 cups vegetable stock

2 cep mushrooms, finely sliced

200 ml/¾ cup double/heavy cream

sea salt and freshly ground black pepper

for the garnish

chopped fresh parsley

fresh thyme leaves

truffle oil, for drizzling (optional)

SERVES 6

Melt about three-quarters of the butter in a large saucepan and cook the onions, garlic, pumpkin and squash until soft. Add the stock to the pan and bring to a boil. Reduce the heat and simmer for about 15 minutes, until the pumpkin and squash are cooked.

Take the pan off the heat and blitz the mixture to a purée with a stick blender.

In a frying pan/skillet, heat the remaining butter and fry the ceps very gently for a few minutes, until softened but without colouring. Add the ceps to the soup and stir in the cream, then season to taste with salt and black pepper.

Ladle the soup into bowls and serve garnished with a sprinkle of fresh parsley and thyme leaves and a little drizzle of truffle oil, if you wish.

roasted squash, chickpea & chorizo soup

450 g/4 cups squash, peeled, deseeded and cut into 1–2-cm/½–¾ in. dice

5 tablespoons olive oil

1–2 pinches dried chilli/hot red pepper flakes, crushed

1 large onion, finely diced

2 carrots, diced

2 celery sticks/ribs, sliced

180 g/6 oz. chorizo or other spicy cooking sausage, peeled and diced

1 fresh red chilli/chile, deseeded and finely chopped

2 garlic cloves, thinly sliced

a small of bunch of flat-leaf parsley, stalks and leaves separated, both chopped

1 teaspoon each crushed cumin seeds and coriander seeds

2 tablespoons chopped oregano or 1½ teaspoons dried

1 x 200-g/7-oz can chopped tomatoes

1 x 400-g/14-oz can chickpeas, drained and rinsed

1.2 litres/5 cups vegetable stock

freshly squeezed lemon juice, to taste (optional)

sea salt and freshly ground black pepper

SERVES 4–5

Roasting the squash adds depth of flavour and sweetness to this rustic soup, which warms the soul with its brick red and orange colours and robust, spicy flavours. Serve it with good crusty bread and all you need is a salad afterwards for a complete meal.

Preheat the oven to 190°C (375°F) Gas 5. Put the squash on a baking sheet and toss with 2 tablespoons of oil. Season with salt and pepper and sprinkle over the chilli/hot pepper flakes. Roast in the preheated oven, stirring once or twice, until tender and browned, about 35–40 minutes.

Meanwhile, heat the remaining oil in a large saucepan and add the onion with a pinch of salt. Turn the heat to low, cover and cook gently, stirring occasionally, for 10–15 minutes until tender. Add the carrots, celery and chorizo and cook, uncovered, for a further 5–7 minutes until beginning to brown. Add the fresh chilli/chile, garlic, chopped parsley stalks and crushed spices. Stir-fry for another 4–5 minutes. Add the oregano, tomatoes, chickpeas and stock and bring to the boil. Reduce the heat and simmer gently for 10–12 minutes until the vegetables are tender. Stir in the roasted squash.

Process or liquidize about half the soup to give a coarse purée, then return it to the saucepan and reheat. Check the seasoning, adding more salt and/or lemon juice to taste. Finally, stir in the chopped parsley leaves and serve piping hot.

roast pumpkin & apple soup

TOPPED WITH MAPLE NUT CRUMBLE

This warming and comforting soup is a surefire winner as a starter for a winter's dinner or served with crusty bread for a satisfying lunch. It's delicious on its own, but to make it truly memorable for your guests, top with the nutty crumble.

4 Pink Lady apples, peeled, cored and roughly chopped into eighths

1.4 kg/11½ cups pumpkin, skinned and chopped into pieces the same size as the apple

2 onions, quartered

a piece of fresh ginger the size of a wine cork, peeled and sliced

6 garlic cloves, skin on

4 tablespoons olive oil

1.5 litres/6 cups warm chicken or vegetable stock

2 tablespoons double/heavy cream and maple syrup

salt and freshly ground black pepper

maple nut crumble

120 g/¾ cup mixed pumpkin seeds, hazelnuts, almonds, macadamia nuts

1 teaspoon salt

80 g/scant ½ cup (caster/superfine) sugar

SERVES 4

Preheat the oven to 200°C (400°F) Gas 6.

Put the apple, pumpkin, onion, ginger and garlic in a roasting pan. Drizzle with olive oil and season with salt and pepper. Roast for 45 minutes, until golden. (Roast for another 30 minutes if you have time. This will give more colour and sweetness.)

Remove from the oven. Squeeze the garlic from its skins and transfer the flesh to a saucepan. Add the pumpkin, apple, ginger and onion and any juices from the roasting pan. Pour over the warm stock and stir to combine. Process with a stick blender until very smooth. Season with salt and pepper.

For the nut crumble: dry-toast the nuts and seeds in a frying pan/skillet. Pour them onto a baking sheet lined with baking parchment and sprinkle with salt.

Put the sugar in a pan and place over medium heat. Swirl the pan, rather than stirring, to mix the sugar as it melts. Cook until all the sugar has melted and has turned a light gold colour. Pour the molten sugar over the top of the nuts. Be careful: the sugar will be very, very hot. Transfer the baking sheet to the freezer and chill for 30 minutes. Chop the praline on the baking parchment into rough pebbles.

Heat the soup through before serving, topped with the nut crumble, cream and maple syrup.

butternut squash & orange soup

WITH GINGER

55 g/4 tablespoons butter

2 onions, diced

1 large butternut squash (or pumpkin), peeled, deseeded and diced

3 large carrots, peeled and sliced

1 leek, white only, sliced

a good pinch of cumin seeds

a good pinch of garam masala

a good pinch of ground turmeric

a pinch of saffron fronds (optional)

a good pinch of ground ginger or a 1-cm/½-in. piece of fresh ginger, peeled and grated

freshly grated zest and freshly squeezed juice of 1 large orange

1.5 litres/6 cups vegetable stock

350 ml/1⅓ cups sour cream

sea salt and freshly ground black pepper

To garnish

toasted pumpkin seeds

sprigs of fresh thyme or dill

SERVES 6

The warming spice and silky smooth texture of the butternut squash or pumpkin is a wonderful golden nectar. This soup is great for any occasion, especially in the winter months, but it works particularly well for a Halloween gathering – you could even serve it from a hollowed-out pumpkin shell.

Melt the butter in a large saucepan and add the onions, squash, carrots and leek. Toss the vegetables in the butter and cook over medium heat for a few minutes, then stir in the spices and orange zest so that the vegetables are evenly coated. Pour over the stock, cover the pan and simmer for about 15–20 minutes, until the vegetables are tender.

Draw the pan off the heat and blend with a stick blender until very smooth. Stir in the orange juice and sour cream and season to taste with salt and black pepper.

Ladle the soup into bowls and sprinkle with toasted pumpkin seeds and fresh thyme leaves to garnish before serving.

creamy pumpkin soup

WITH GINGER & HONEY

The addition of spicy honey makes this smooth, creamy soup quite unique. It's a great winter soup and, if it's not a pumpkin time of year, you can simply use butternut squash instead.

3 tablespoons olive oil

1 tablespoon butter

1 onion, chopped

50 g/2-in. piece of fresh ginger, peeled and chopped

2 teaspoons coriander seeds

2 teaspoons fennel seeds

1 kg/2 lbs. 4 oz. peeled and deseeded pumpkin flesh, roughly chopped

1 litre/4 cups vegetable stock

150 ml/⅔ cup double/heavy cream

2–3 tablespoons runny honey

1–2 teaspoons finely chopped fresh red chilli/chile

SERVES 4–6

Heat the oil and butter in a heavy-based saucepan, stir in the onion, ginger, coriander seeds and fennel seeds and sauté for 2–3 minutes, until the onion begins to colour. Toss in the pumpkin, stirring to coat it in the onion and ginger, then pour in the stock. Bring the stock to the boil, then reduce the heat, cover the pan and cook gently for about 25 minutes, until the pumpkin is very tender.

Purée the soup with a stick blender, or whizz it in an electric blender, and tip it back into the pan. Simmer the soup over a low heat, season well with salt and pepper and stir in the cream.

Heat the honey in a small pan and stir in the chopped chilli/chile.

Ladle the soup into individual bowls, swirl a little of the honey onto the surface of each one and serve immediately.

pumpkin, carrot & red lentil soup

70 g/½ cup chopped leek (white part) or onion

4 tablespoons olive oil

a pinch of sea salt

200 g/1⅔ cups peeled and seeded pumpkin or squash wedges cut into 3–4-cm/1¼–1½-in. pieces

120 g/1 cup carrot cut into 2–3-cm/¼–1¼-in. pieces

1 teaspoon vegetable bouillon powder

¼ teaspoon ground turmeric

4 garlic cloves, crushed

2 bay leaves

3 dried tomato halves, chopped

2 tablespoons cooking wine

150 g/¾ cup dried red lentils, washed and drained

7-cm/2¾-in. strip of kombu seaweed

1 litre/4 cups water

a squeeze of lemon juice

a little crushed black pepper

1 tablespoon umeboshi vinegar

SERVES 4

The addition of lentils makes this a more substantial and filling soup than most, so you might want to skip the bread accompaniment. Vibrant and velvety, this is definitely a soup you will make time and again. When pumpkins aren't in season, substitute with squash.

In a large saucepan, sauté the leek or onions in the olive oil with the salt, uncovered, until they're soft and transparent. Add the pumpkin or squash and carrot and sauté until the veggies start to 'sweat'. Add the bouillon powder, turmeric, garlic, bay leaves and tomatoes and stir. Next, pour in the wine and let the mixture boil. Now it's time to add the lentils, kombu and water.

Turn up the heat, cover and bring to a boil. Then, lower the heat and let simmer for about 25–30 minutes or until the lentils and vegetables are completely tender (if pressure cooking, you'll only need to let it cook for 15 minutes).

At this point, remove the bay leaves. Use a handheld blender to purée the soup and make it creamy, or leave as it is if you prefer it chunky and more stew-like. Add the lemon juice, crushed pepper, and umeboshi vinegar and stir. Taste and add more spices if desired. You can add more hot water if the soup seems too thick, and it will definitely thicken as it cools.

spicy pumpkin & coconut soup

WITH GINGER & LIME

This beautiful orange and green soup with its sweet-sour flavour and spicy kick makes an exotic start to a special meal. Despite the richness of the coconut milk, the sharpness of the lime keeps it tasting light. You can use any orange-fleshed winter squash or cooking pumpkin for this recipe.

2 tablespoons sunflower oil

750 g/6¼ cups pumpkin or squash, peeled, deseeded and cut into chunks

a bunch of spring onions/ scallions, chopped

a 5-cm/2-in. piece of fresh ginger, peeled and chopped

2 garlic cloves, chopped

2–3 fresh red chillies/chiles, deseeded and chopped, plus extra slices to garnish

2 lemongrass stalks, spilt lengthways

a large bunch of coriander/ cilantro, stalks and leaves separated

1.2 litres/5 cups vegetable or chicken stock

1 x 400-ml/14-fl. oz. can coconut milk

2–3 tablespoons Thai fish sauce

freshly squeezed juice of 1–2 limes

crème fraîche or sour cream, to serve

SERVES 6

Heat the oil in a large saucepan and, over low heat, sweat the pumpkin and onions with a pinch of salt until soft but not browned, about 15–20 minutes.

Meanwhile, put the ginger, garlic, chillies/chiles, lemongrass and coriander/cilantro stalks in another saucepan with the stock and simmer gently, covered, for 20–25 minutes. Let the stock cool slightly, then liquidize and sieve into the saucepan with the pumpkin mixture, pressing hard on the contents of the sieve/ strainer to extract maximum flavour. Discard the debris in the sieve/strainer, then process or liquidize the liquid again with the pumpkin mixture until smooth.

Return the soup to the rinsed-out saucepan, add the coconut milk, 2 tablespoons fish sauce and the juice of 1 lime, then reheat, stirring all the time, to just below boiling point. Adjust the seasoning, adding more fish sauce and lime juice to taste. Chop most of the coriander/cilantro leaves finely and stir into the soup (keep a few roughly chopped leaves to scatter over the soup at the end). Heat for a few minutes, but do not allow to boil.

Serve piping hot, topped with a spoonful of crème fraîche and scattered with the reserved chopped coriander/cilantro leaves and/or some extra red chilli/chile slices.

miso pumpkin soup

This hearty soup really is full of goodness. The pumpkin provides beta-carotene, one of the most important antioxidants, and there are vital health-giving enzymes in the miso paste. It's important to choose your miso carefully to get just the right flavour – see below.

2 tablespoons dark sesame oil

60 g/½ cup diced white onion

60 g /½ cup peeled, seeded and cubed pumpkin, squash or carrots

4 garlic cloves, crushed

1 tablespoon crushed fresh ginger

800 ml/3½ cups bouillon or cold water (unsalted)

1 tablespoon barley or rice miso

¼ sheet toasted nori, cut into small pieces

1 tablespoon chopped flat-leaf parsley

1 teaspoon toasted sesame seeds

sea salt

SERVES 2–3

Place the sesame oil in a saucepan and sauté the onions for a minute or so before adding the pumpkin (or squash or carrot) along with the garlic, ginger and a pinch of salt. Sauté the mixture for a little longer, and then add the cold water or bouillon and cover. Bring to a boil, lower the heat and cook until the vegetables become tender.

Take 60 ml/¼ cup of the hot soup and put it in a small bowl. Now add the tablespoon of miso to it. Purée the miso really well with a fork, until it has completely melted. Put the miso liquid back into the soup. Taste and adjust the seasoning. Turn off the heat, cover and let the soup sit for a couple of minutes. Serve sprinkled with the pieces of nori, a sprinkling of sesame seeds, the chopped parsley and sesame seeds.

Don't forget that you can combine different kinds of miso in the same soup! Since hatcho (soya/soy bean) miso is of high quality but has a strong taste, try to combine ½ tablespoon soya/soy miso with ½ tablespoon barley miso, to get all the benefits of both kinds of soya/soy bean paste. In warmer weather, substitute darker miso pastes with sweet white miso, which is a lot milder.

pumpkin & coconut laksa

1 delica pumpkin or butternut squash, peeled, halved and deseeded

2 tablespoons olive oil

sea salt

2 tablespoons vegetable oil

4 shallots, thinly sliced

4 tablespoons laksa curry paste

3 tablespoons coconut palm sugar or pure maple syrup

1½ teaspoons sea salt

zest and juice of 1 lime (about 2 tablespoons), plus another lime, cut into wedges, to serve

2 tablespoons tamarind paste (alternatively use another 2 tablespoons of lime juice)

2 x 400-ml/14-fl. oz. cans coconut milk

400 ml/1⅔ cups vegetable stock

a few spinach leaves

200 g/6½ oz. rice noodles

½ a red onion, sliced

1 fresh red chilli/chile, deseeded and thinly sliced

small handful of fresh mint leaves

SERVES 4

This vibrant soup is by turns sour, sweet, salty and spicy. Delica pumpkins, with their emerald green skin and bright orange flesh are great, but if they aren't available you can use any kind of squash instead.

Preheat the oven to 180°C (360°F) Gas 4. Cut the pumpkin halves into 3-cm/1¼-in. chunks, drizzle with the olive oil, season with salt and roast in the preheated oven for 30 minutes until cooked through.

Place a large pot with 2 tablespoons of vegetable oil over medium heat. Add in the shallots and stir-fry for a few minutes until softened. Turn down the heat, add in the curry paste and cook gently for 5 minutes until fragrant. Add in the sugar or maple syrup, salt, lime zest and juice and tamarind paste. Cook for another few minutes until the sugar has dissolved and everything is sizzling. Add in the coconut milk and stock and bring to a boil. Reduce the heat, and simmer briskly for 10 minutes.

Taste the soup and if necessary adjust the seasoning with a little more salt, lime juice or coconut palm sugar. You should be able to taste all the sour, salty, sweet elements quite strongly. Add in the cooked pumpkin and the spinach leaves, stirring into the sauce until slightly wilted.

Cook the noodles according to the packet instructions. Ladle the soup into bowls and then add in a mound of noodles. Scatter over some of the red onion, chilli/chile and mint leaves and serve immediately with the lime wedges to squeeze over.

casseroles & curries

healing azuki bean & pumpkin stew

WITH AMARANTH

Requiring little effort but with great rewards, this well-balanced, nourishing stew should be top of your list when you need comfort food. The consistency is rich and creamy and the taste slightly sweet, satisfying your taste buds and leaving you feeling that little bit healthier.

200 g/1 cup dried azuki beans

1 litre/4 cups cold water

180 g/1½ cups peeled, seeded and cubed hokkaido or kabocha pumpkin

70 g/⅓ cup amaranth

2 tablespoons soy sauce

½ tablespoon umeboshi vinegar

½ teaspoon ground turmeric

½ teaspoon sea salt

SERVES 2–3

Cover the azuki beans with the water in a saucepan and soak overnight (this is not necessary but will speed up the cooking).

Bring the beans to a boil in the soaking water, then add the pumpkin and cook, half-covered, over a low heat, until the azuki are half-done (about 30 minutes).

Add the amaranth and cook until both the azuki and amaranth are soft (another 20–30 minutes).

Season with the remaining ingredients and adjust the thickness by adding hot water, if necessary.

- **40 g/3 tablespoons butter**
- **3 tablespoons olive oil**
- **1 teaspoon each crushed cumin seeds and coriander seeds**
- **a piece of cinnamon stick**
- **2 large onions, halved and thinly sliced**
- **2 garlic cloves, chopped**
- **1 teaspoon chopped fresh ginger**
- **1 fresh green chilli/chile, deseeded and chopped, plus a little extra to taste**
- **4 chicken leg joints, cut in 2, or a chicken, jointed into 8 pieces**
- **2–3 bay leaves**
- **2 teaspoons honey**
- **2 tablespoons chopped preserved lemon (discard any pips), plus a little extra to taste**
- **a small bunch of coriander/cilantro, stalks and leaves separated**
- **400 ml/2 cups chicken stock**
- **½ teaspoon smoked Spanish paprika (pimentón)**
- **750 g/6¼ cups squash, peeled, deseeded and cut into small wedges or slices**
- **a good pinch of saffron threads**
- **50 g/1¾ oz. blanched almonds, fried in a little butter until light brown**
- **sea salt and freshly ground black pepper**

SERVES 4

chicken & butternut squash tagine WITH SAFFRON

This Moroccan-inspired stew is heady with the scent of saffron and sharp with lemon, all of which works so well with the sweet density of the roasted squash. It is delicious served with buttered couscous.

Heat the butter and 1 tablespoon of the oil in a flameproof casserole or heavy-based frying pan/skillet. Add the spices and cook over low heat for 2–3 minutes, then add the onions, garlic, ginger and chilli/chile and cook gently for 5–6 minutes more. Add the chicken and turn it in the juices for 1–2 minutes – do not let it brown. Add the bay leaves, honey, preserved lemon and chopped coriander/cilantro stalks. Add the stock, ¼ teaspoon salt, black pepper to taste and paprika. Bring to the boil then stir well, cover and cook very gently for about 45–50 minutes until the chicken is very tender.

Meanwhile, preheat the oven to 190°C (375°F) Gas 5. Toss the squash in the remaining oil, season and roast on a baking sheet until browned and tender, about 35–40 minutes. Soak the saffron in 2 tablespoons hot water and chop the coriander/cilantro leaves.

When the chicken is done, transfer it to a serving dish and keep warm. Turn the heat up under the casserole and reduce the liquid by about half, then add the saffron and most of the coriander/cilantro. Cook for a few minutes, then taste. Adjust the seasoning, adding more chilli/chile or preserved lemon to taste. Stir in the roasted squash and heat through. Spoon the squash and sauce over the chicken, sprinkle with the remaining coriander/cilantro and almonds and serve immediately.

pumpkin, apple & sultana tagine

2 tablespoons olive oil

700 g/6 cups pumpkin, skinned, deseeded and cut into bite-sized chunks

2 apples, peeled, cored and cut into bite-sized chunks

2 tablespoons sultanas/golden raisins or raisins

1 teaspoon smoked paprika

1 quantity chermoula (below)

sea salt and freshly ground black pepper

a small bunch of fresh mint leaves, finely shredded, to garnish

for the chermoula

2–3 garlic cloves, roughly chopped

1 fresh red chilli/chile, deseeded and roughly chopped

1–2 teaspoons cumin seeds

1 teaspoon sea salt

big bunch of fresh coriander/ cilantro leaves, finely chopped

a pinch of saffron threads, soaked in water

freshly squeezed juice of 1 lemon

3–4 tablespoons olive oil

SERVES 4–6

The combination of pumpkin and apple with the tangy, spicy chermoula makes this a delicious accompaniment to plain grilled or roasted dishes.

To make the chermoula, use a mortar and pestle to pound the garlic with the chilli/chile, cumin seeds and salt to a coarse paste. Add the chopped coriander/cilantro and pound again to as smooth a paste as you can get. Stir in the saffron, along with its soaking water, and the lemon juice and olive oil.

Heat the oil in the base of a tagine or in a heavy-based saucepan, toss in the pumpkin and sauté for 1–2 minutes. Add the apple and sultanas/golden raisins and cook for a further 1–2 minutes, until the sultanas/golden raisins plump up. Sprinkle in the paprika, stir in the chermoula and pour in enough water to cover the base of the tagine. Bring the water to the boil, put on the lid and cook over a medium heat for 20–25 minutes, until the pumpkin is tender.

Season the tagine with salt and pepper, garnish with a little shredded mint, and serve.

Moroccan honey-glazed pumpkin

WITH SPICES

When root vegetables and members of the squash family, such as sweet potatoes, turnips, butternut and pumpkins, are cooked with honey and spices their sweet flesh remains succulent and marries well with the flavours. This is the perfect side dish to complement roasted meats.

700 g/6 cups pumpkin flesh, with skin and seeds removed

50 g/3½ tablespoons butter

2–3 tablespoons runny honey

2 cinnamon sticks

3–4 cloves

1 teaspoon ground ginger

½ teaspoon cayenne

a small bunch of fresh coriander/cilantro, finely chopped

sea salt and freshly ground black pepper

an ovenproof baking dish

SERVES 4

Preheat the oven to 180°C (350°F) Gas 4.

Put the pumpkin in a steamer and cook for about 10 minutes, until the flesh is tender but still firm. Tip the steamed flesh into an ovenproof dish.

Melt the butter in a saucepan and stir in the honey. Add the cinnamon sticks, cloves, ground ginger and cayenne and season to taste with salt and pepper. Pour the mixture over the pumpkin, then bake in the preheated oven for 15–20 minutes.

Tip the glazed pumpkin onto a serving plate, remove the cinnamon and cloves, then sprinkle with the coriander/cilantro. Serve warm as a side dish to roasted or grilled/broiled chicken or meat.

beef with butternut squash

& SZECHUAN PEPPER

Fragrant and mouth-tingling Szechuan peppercorns give a wonderful flavour and aroma to tender sirloin steak and sweet, creamy butternut squash. If you can't find Szechuan peppercorns in the spice section of your supermarket, visit your nearest oriental grocery store.

600 g/1 lb. 5 oz. sirloin steak, trimmed of fat and thinly sliced against the grain

400 g/3⅓ cups butternut squash flesh, diced

2 tablespoons peanut oil

2 garlic cloves, thinly sliced

1 tablespoon finely grated fresh ginger

3 tablespoons sweet chilli/ chili sauce

2 tablespoons dark soy sauce

a small bunch of coriander/ cilantro leaves, roughly chopped

½ fresh red chilli/chile, deseeded and thinly sliced, to garnish

for the marinade

2 tablespoons dark soy sauce

1 tablespoon crushed Szechuan peppercorns

SERVES 4–6

Combine the marinade ingredients in a bowl, stir in the beef, cover and marinate in the refrigerator for 20–30 minutes.

Bring a saucepan of lightly salted water to the boil, then add the butternut squash. Bring back to the boil and blanch for about 5 minutes, or until tender, then drain well and set aside.

Heat the peanut oil in a wok or large frying pan/skillet until hot. Add the beef and stir-fry over high heat for 3–4 minutes, or until sealed. Remove the beef from the wok and set aside.

Add the garlic and ginger to the wok and stir-fry for 3–4 minutes, or until golden. Add the butternut squash with the sweet chilli/chili sauce, soy sauce and 1 tablespoon water. Bring to the boil, then reduce the heat and simmer gently for 2 minutes. Return the beef to the wok and stir-fry until cooked through.

Remove from the heat and stir in the chopped coriander/cilantro. Divide between 4–6 bowls and garnish with the sliced chilli/chile.

1 kg/2 lb. 3 oz. braising or stewing steak

1 teaspoon ground allspice

1 rounded teaspoon smoked Spanish paprika (pimentón)

4–6 tablespoons olive oil

4 garlic cloves, finely chopped

a small bunch of oregano

2 medium onions, sliced

2–3 fresh red chillies/chiles, deseeded and cut into thin strips, plus extra, finely sliced, to garnish

1 teaspoon cumin seeds, lightly crushed

1 x 400-g/14-fl. oz. can chopped tomatoes

750 ml/3½ cups beef stock

a small piece of cinnamon stick and a strip of orange zest

600 g/5 cups orange-fleshed squash or pumpkin, such as butternut, kabocha or calabaza, peeled, deseeded and cut into chunks

2 red (bell) peppers, deseeded and cut into chunks

brown sugar, to taste (optional)

200 g/1½ cups fresh sweetcorn kernels

20 g/¾ oz. dark, bitter chocolate (70% cocoa minimum)

sea salt and freshly ground black pepper

SERVES 6

beef stew with squash

Make use of your hollowed-out pumpkin to serve this tasty stew. Packed with spicy flavour, it is given added richness by the last-minute addition of dark chocolate.

Cut the steak into 5-cm/2-in. pieces, discarding any excess fat and put in a sealable bag with the ground allspice and half the paprika. Add 2 tablespoons of the oil, half the garlic, a little salt and some black pepper. Chop 1 tablespoon oregano finely and add it to the bag. Seal the bag, massage the marinade into the beef and let marinate in the refrigerator for several hours.

When ready to cook, preheat the oven to 160°C (325°F) Gas 3.

Scrape the marinade off the beef and reserve it. Dry the meat on kitchen paper. Heat the remaining oil in a frying pan/skillet and brown the meat on all sides. Do this in batches, putting the beef into a flameproof casserole as you cook it. Reduce the heat, add the onions to the pan with a pinch of salt and cook gently for 10–15 minutes until soft and sweet. Add the chillies/chiles, remaining garlic and the crushed cumin and fry for another 3–4 minutes. Add the marinade and remaining paprika followed by the tomatoes and cook over medium heat for a few minutes. Add the stock, cinnamon and orange zest, bring to the boil and pour over the beef in the casserole. Cover with a sheet of greaseproof paper and the lid to make a tight seal and cook in the preheated oven for 1½ hours.

Stir in the squash and red (bell) peppers. Check and adjust the seasoning, adding salt, pepper or a pinch of brown sugar as necessary. Cook for a further 30 minutes at 180°C (350°F) Gas 4, then stir in the sweetcorn and cook for another 25–30 minutes. Make sure the squash is fully cooked. Remove the casserole from the oven and set over medium heat. Chop some of the remaining oregano leaves to give about 1–2 teaspoons. Stir the dark chocolate and chopped oregano into the stew. Let it bubble for a few minutes, then serve scattered with the extra chilli/chile and a few sprigs of the remaining oregano.

fish, pumpkin & coconut curry

1 medium pumpkin, peeled, deseeded and sliced

4 tablespoons sunflower oil

5-cm/2-in. piece of fresh ginger, peeled and chopped

4 garlic cloves, chopped

a small bunch of coriander/cilantro, stalks and leaves separated

3–4 red chillies/chiles, deseeded

1 large onion, sliced

300 g/10 oz. tomatoes, skinned, deseeded and chopped

400 ml/1¾ cup fish stock

2 green (bell) peppers, deseeded and sliced

1 x 400-g/14-oz. can coconut milk

2–4 teaspoons tamarind paste

900 g/2 lbs. thick, white fish fillets, cut into chunks

650 g/1 lb. 7 oz. shelled, uncooked prawns/shrimp, deveined

sea salt and freshly ground black pepper

for the spice mix

4 cloves

1 teaspoon coriander seeds

2 teaspoons cumin seeds

½ teaspoon black peppercorns

1 teaspoon ground turmeric

SERVES 4–6

The sweet, rich flavour of roasted pumpkin works so well with the spices in this light, fragrant curry. The fish you use needs to be one that will cut into chunks and not break up on cooking – monkfish is good.

Preheat the oven to 200°C (400°F) Gas 6.

Toss the pumpkin with 2 tablespoons of the oil and some salt and pepper. Transfer to a baking sheet and roast in the preheated oven, stirring once or twice, until browned and tender (about 35 minutes).

Meanwhile, in a small dry frying pan/skillet over medium heat, toast the cloves, coriander seeds and half the cumin seeds for 2–3 minutes until fragrant. Let cool, then grind in a mill or mortar and pestle with the black peppercorns to make a powder. Stir in the ground turmeric. Blend together the ginger, garlic, coriander/cilantro stalks and 2–3 chillies/chiles with 3 tablespoons water to form a paste, then blend in 2 teaspoons of the dry spice mixture.

In a saucepan, very gently fry the onion in the remaining oil with a pinch of salt for 10 minutes until softened but not browned. Add the remaining cumin seeds and fry for another 3–4 minutes, then add the ginger paste, turn up the heat and stir-fry for 4–5 minutes until the liquid evaporates. Add the tomatoes and cook again for 3–4 minutes until the mixture looks dry. Stir in the stock and green (bell) peppers and cook for 10 minutes.

Add the coconut milk and 2 teaspoons tamarind paste. Let it bubble gently for a few minutes, then stir in the seasoning and more tamarind to taste. Stir in the pumpkin and fish and let it gently cook for 5 minutes, then add the prawns/shrimp and cook until they turn pink.

Add more of the spice mixture to taste, stir in most of the chopped coriander/cilantro leaves and transfer to a serving dish. Sprinkle with the remaining coriander/cilantro and red chilli/chile, thinly sliced. Serve immediately.

Thai pumpkin & vegetable curry

coconut or avocado oil, for frying

1 onion, finely diced

1 yellow (bell) pepper, deseeded and chopped into thin strips

1 tablespoon grated fresh ginger

1 tablespoon freshly chopped coriander/cilantro stems (leaves reserved for serving)

2 tablespoons red Thai curry paste, or more to taste

235 ml/1 cup vegetable stock

250 g/2 cups pumpkin or butternut squash, peeled and cut into chunks

1 x 400-g/14-oz. can coconut milk

1 tablespoon tamari

1 crown of broccoli, cut into small florets

130 g/1 cup frozen shelled edamame beans/green peas, thawed

salt, to taste

cooked brown rice or quinoa, to serve (optional)

SERVES 4

This coconut-based curry is so packed with good vegetables that no one will miss the meat. There's hearty winter squash, (bell) peppers, broccoli and edamame beans (or green peas) for a nutritious and colourful curry that is pleasing on the eye.

Heat a thin layer of oil in a large saucepan over a medium-high heat. Add the onion, (bell) pepper and a pinch of salt and cook for 5 minutes, stirring occasionally.

Add the ginger, coriander/cilantro stems and curry paste and cook, stirring, for 1 minute. Add the vegetable stock and the butternut squash or pumpkin and stir to combine. Reduce the heat to medium, cover with a lid and cook for 7–8 minutes.

Stir in the coconut milk, tamari, broccoli and edamame beans or peas, cover with a lid and bring to a boil. Reduce the heat and simmer for another 3–5 minutes until the butternut squash and broccoli are tender and easily pierced with a fork. Remove from the heat and allow to stand for 5 minutes uncovered.

Taste for seasoning, adding more salt if needed, and serve warm over cooked rice or quinoa (if desired) and top with fresh coriander/cilantro leaves to serve.

pasta & rice

tagliatelle with pan-fried pumpkin

& RED PEPPER OIL

The trick to this recipe is to let the red pepper and chillies/chiles gently release their colour and flavour into the oil by roasting them in a low oven for an hour. The pumpkin makes this a wonderfully warming pasta dish for a cold winter's evening.

1 tablespoon light olive oil

400 g/3⅓ cups pumpkin or winter squash, peeled, deseeded and chopped into 2.5 cm/1 in. pieces

400 g/14 oz. pappardelle, tagliatelle or any other ribbon pasta

finely grated zest and juice of unwaxed lemon

50 g/1¾ oz. wild rocket/arugula leaves

1 large handful of chopped fresh flat-leaf parsley

sea salt and freshly ground black pepper

for the red pepper oil

1 small red (bell) pepper, sliced

6 large red chillies/chiles, sliced

1 small red onion, sliced

4 garlic cloves, peeled but left whole

1 teaspoon cumin seeds

65 ml/2 fl. oz. olive oil

SERVES 4

Preheat the oven to 180°C (350°F) Gas 4.

Put the red (bell) pepper, chillies/chiles, onion, garlic, cumin seeds and 2 tablespoons of the olive oil in a roasting pan. Cook in the preheated oven for 1 hour, turning often. Transfer the contents of the roasting pan to a food processor while still hot. Add the remaining oil and whizz until smooth. Let cool, then pour the mixture into a clean and dry screwtop jar.

Heat the light olive oil in a frying pan/skillet set over high and add the pumpkin. Cook for 10 minutes, turning often, until each piece is golden brown all over. Meanwhile, cook the pasta according to the packet instructions and drain well. Put it in a large bowl and add 2–3 tablespoons of the red pepper oil. Add the cooked pumpkin, lemon zest and juice, rocket/arugula and parsley and toss to combine. Season well with salt and pepper and serve immediately.

Note: The remaining oil will keep for 1 week when stored in an airtight jar in the refrigerator. It can be added to tomato-based sauces and soups for extra flavour.

orange vegetable & spring onion pilau

Rich in spices and healthy vegetables, this vibrant rice dish is the perfect way to add colour and flavour to a dinner plate. It makes a great side dish, but is substantial and satisfying enough to serve as a main meal too.

2 tablespoons light olive oil

3 large spring onions/ scallions, chopped

2 garlic cloves, chopped

1 tablespoon finely grated fresh ginger

1 large red chilli/chile, finely chopped

1 teaspoon ground coriander

1 teaspoon ground cumin

1 teaspoon turmeric

50 g/1¾ oz. flaked/slivered almonds

300 g/1½ cups basmati rice

1 carrot, cut into large chunks

200 g/1½ cups pumpkin or squash, peeled, deseeded and cut into wedges

1 small sweet potato, peeled and cut into thick half-circles

freshly squeezed juice of 1 lime

1 handful of fresh coriander/ cilantro leaves, chopped

SERVES 4

Put the oil in a heavy-based saucepan set over high heat. Add the spring onion/scallions, garlic, ginger and chilli/chile and cook for 5 minutes, stirring often. Add the spices and almonds and cook for a further 5 minutes, until the spices become aromatic and look very dark in the pan.

Add the rice and cook for a minute, stirring well to coat the rice in the spices. Add the carrot, pumpkin and sweet potato to the pan. Pour in 600 ml/3 cups water and stir well, loosening any grains of rice that are stuck to the bottom of the pan. Bring to the boil, then reduce the heat to low, cover with a tight-fitting lid and cook for 25 minutes, stirring occasionally.

Add the lime juice and coriander/cilantro, stir well to combine and serve.

pasta with pan-fried squash & walnut

& PARSLEY SAUCE

This lovely and unusual pasta dish is well-suited to the season of mists and mellow fruitfulness, when walnuts and all kinds of orange-fleshed squashes will be at their best. Traditionally, a version of this walnut sauce is served with pappardelle pasta in northern Italy, but it is good with other shapes too.

150 g/5¼ oz. fresh walnut halves

2–3 fat garlic cloves, peeled

5 tablespoons olive oil

1 tablespoon walnut oil

5 tablespoons crème fraîche or sour cream

a small bunch of flat-leaf parsley

freshly squeezed lemon juice, to taste

650 g/5½ cups prepared squash, cut into 1 cm/½ in. thick slices or chunks

1–2 pinches dried chilli/hot red pepper flakes, crushed

400 g/14 oz. pasta of your choice

freshly grated nutmeg, to taste

sea salt and freshly ground black pepper

freshly grated Parmesan, to serve

SERVES 4

Preheat the oven to 180°C (350°F) Gas 4.

Put the walnuts on a baking sheet and toast them in the preheated oven for 5–6 minutes, making sure they don't burn. Turn them onto a dry, clean tea towel/dishtowel and rub vigorously to remove as much of the skin as possible. Chop a third of the nuts roughly and set aside, then put the remaining nuts in a food processor.

Blanch the garlic in boiling water for 2–3 minutes, drain and rinse. Put the garlic in the processor with the walnuts, add 2 tablespoons olive oil, the walnut oil and cream. Whizz to make a paste. Set aside a third of the parsley, then whizz the remaining two-thirds into the sauce. Chop the reserved parsley and set aside. Leave the sauce in the processor until needed.

In a large frying pan/skillet, heat the remaining olive oil over medium heat, add the squash and chilli/hot red pepper flakes and cook, turning the squash now and then, until it is tender and lightly browned, about 10–12 minutes. Meanwhile, bring a large saucepan of salted water to the boil and cook the pasta according to the packet instructions.

When the pasta is cooked, drain, reserving 4–5 tablespoons of the cooking water. Whizz enough of this water into the sauce to make it creamy, then season with salt, pepper and a little nutmeg. Toss the pasta with the squash, remaining walnuts and parsley and a little of the sauce. Serve the Parmesan and remaining sauce at the table.

butternut squash & sage mac & cheese

Earthy sage and sweet butternut squash are a match made in heaven – and they taste even better topped with lashings of cream and melted cheese. This comforting dish is perfect served as a main meal or as an accompaniment to roasted meats.

500 g/1 lb. macaroni

1 large (or 1 kg/7 cups) butternut squash, skinned, deseeded and cubed

3 tablespoons vegetable oil

30 g/2 tablespoons butter

2 shallots, finely chopped

650 ml/2¾ cups double/heavy cream

leaves from a few sprigs of fresh sage, finely chopped

100 g/1½ cups grated Padano or Parmesan

100 g/1½ cups grated Cheddar cheese

50 g/1 cup fresh breadcrumbs

fine sea salt and freshly ground black pepper

SERVES 6–8

Cook the macaroni according to the packet instructions.

Preheat the oven to 200°C (400°F) Gas 6.

Arrange the squash in a single layer on a baking sheet. Sprinkle over 2 tablespoons of the oil and toss to coat lightly. Roast in the oven for 20–25 minutes until just charred. Remove the squash from the oven and put it in a very large bowl. Season lightly with salt and set aside.

Heat the butter and the remaining oil in a large saucepan. Add the shallots and cook over high heat for 2–3 minutes, or until golden, stirring occasionally. Add the cream, sage and a good pinch of salt and bring to the boil, then reduce the heat. Add the cheeses and stir well to melt.

Preheat the grill/broiler to medium–hot.

Put the cooked macaroni in the bowl with the squash. Pour over the hot cream sauce and mix well. Taste and adjust the seasoning. Transfer the macaroni mixture to a baking dish and spread evenly. Top with a good grinding of black pepper and sprinkle the breadcrumbs evenly over the top.

Grill/broil for 5–10 minutes until the top is crunchy and golden brown. Serve immediately.

pumpkin gnocchi

WITH BUTTERY SAGE BREADCRUMBS

These gnocchi are light and yet deeply satisfying. Don't prepare them too far ahead of cooking or they will become wet and sticky.

a starchy, dry-fleshed pumpkin or squash, such as kabocha or crown prince (about 750 g/6 cups), halved and deseeded

500 g/1 lb. medium floury potatoes, unpeeled, washed and pricked

180 g/1⅓ cups plain/all-purpose flour, sifted with ½ teaspoon baking powder, plus extra flour as needed

50 g/1 cup fine semolina, plus extra for dusting

100 g/1½ cups Parmesan cheese, freshly grated, plus extra to serve

freshly grated nutmeg, to taste

100 g/7 tablespoons unsalted butter

1 garlic clove, peeled and halved

30 g/½ cup white breadcrumbs from day-old bread

10 sage leaves, shredded

sea salt and freshly ground black pepper

SERVES 4

Preheat the oven to 200°C (400°F) Gas 6.

Line a baking sheet with lightly oiled foil. Put the pumpkin, cut-side down, and the potatoes on the sheet. Bake in the preheated oven for 1 hour, until soft. (Check the squash after 40 minutes – if cooked, remove it and continue baking the potatoes.) When cool enough to handle, scrape the squash flesh off the skin and do the same with the potato. Using a mouli-légume or sieve, purée the vegetables into a bowl. Do not use a food processor as it will make the potatoes too gluey. While the puréed vegetables are still warm, work in the flour and semolina using a fork. Add more flour as necessary to make a malleable mixture. Work in half of the Parmesan and season well with salt, pepper and nutmeg.

Dust a work surface with semolina. Take about one-third of the mixture and roll it out to form a long, thin sausage shape about 2 cm/¾ in. thick. Cut into 2.5-cm/1-in. lengths. Roll each piece along the tines of a fork, then in a little semolina and set on a tea towel/dishtowel-covered tray, dusted with more semolina. Repeat with the remaining mixture.

Bring a large saucepan of salted water to the boil. Meanwhile, heat half the butter in a frying pan/skillet over medium heat with the garlic. Let the garlic sizzle for a few minutes, then add the breadcrumbs and half the sage. Fry gently until the breadcrumbs turn crisp and golden brown. Discard the garlic. In a separate pan, melt the remaining butter, add the remaining sage and keep warm.

When the water boils, turn it down to a simmer and cook the gnocchi in batches until they bob to the surface, then cook for 1–2 minutes more. Use a slotted spoon to transfer them to a warmed serving dish. Toss with the butter and sage, then with the breadcrumbs. Serve immediately, offering extra Parmesan.

pumpkin & Gorgonzola risotto

By roasting the pumpkin first, before adding it to the risotto, it retains its deep flavour and unique texture. The salty Gorgonzola, stirred in just before serving, perfectly complements the sweet-tasting pumpkin.

500 g/4 cups peeled and cubed pumpkin

1 tablespoon light olive oil

1 litre/4 cups vegetable stock

2 tablespoons butter

1 leek, halved lengthways and thinly sliced

1 garlic clove, chopped

300 g/1½ cups Arborio (risotto) rice

50 g/1¾ oz. Gorgonzola cheese, crumbled

SERVES 4

Preheat the oven to 180°C (350°F) Gas 4.

Put the pumpkin on a baking sheet, drizzle with the olive oil and roast in the preheated oven for 30 minutes.

Put the stock in a saucepan and heat until gently simmering. Melt the butter in a saucepan over high heat and add the leek and garlic. Cook for 4–5 minutes, stirring often, until the leeks have softened but not browned.

Add the rice to the leeks and stir for 1 minute, until the rice is well coated with oil. Add 125 ml/½ cup of the hot stock to the rice and cook, stirring constantly, until the rice has absorbed most of the liquid. Repeat this process until all the stock has been used, this will take about 20–25 minutes. The rice should be soft but still have a slight bite to the centre.

Add the roasted pumpkin pieces. Remove the pan from the heat, stir in the Gorgonzola and serve immediately.

pumpkin, pancetta, & sage risotto

Despite the name, you can use any well-flavoured winter squash for this recipe. If using pumpkin, preferably find an Italian or French variety such as Tonda, Zucca di Napoli or a Musque de Provence. The common orange Halloween or Cinderella pumpkin can be too stringy and watery.

50 g /3½ tablespoons unsalted butter

2 tablespoons olive oil, plus extra for frying the sage leaves

1 medium sweet yellow onion, finely chopped

1 celery rib/stick, finely chopped

140 g/5 oz. pancetta, cut into lardons

500 g/4 cups prepared squash or pumpkin, diced

4–5 sage leaves, torn, plus a small handful extra to garnish

300 g/1½ cups Arborio or Carnaroli risotto rice

150 ml/⅔ cup dry white wine

1.2 litres/5 cups vegetable or chicken stock

40 g/⅔ cup Parmesan cheese, freshly grated, plus extra to serve

sea salt and freshly ground black pepper

SERVES 4

Heat half the butter and 1 tablespoon of the oil in a deep frying pan/skillet. Add the onion, celery and a pinch of salt. Cover the pan, turn the heat down low and let the onion and celery sweat, stirring once or twice until softened and golden but not browned. Add the pancetta and cook for another 5 minutes before adding the squash. Cook gently, uncovered, until the squash is half cooked, about 6 minutes, adding the torn sage leaves for the last 1–2 minutes.

Add the rice and 1 teaspoon salt to the onion and squash mixture. Cook gently, turning the rice with the buttery vegetables, until it begins to look translucent. Turn up the heat, add the wine and cook at a medium simmer, stirring frequently with a wooden spoon, until the wine has evaporated.

Meanwhile, heat the stock in a large saucepan and keep it hot. When the wine has evaporated, add 2 ladlefuls of the hot stock to the rice mixture and stir until it has all been absorbed by the rice. Continue to add more stock, 1–2 ladlefuls at a time, whilst stirring continuously, as this releases the creamy starch in the rice. Repeat until all the stock has been absorbed and the rice is tender but still al dente, about 16–18 minutes. When cooked, stir in the remaining butter and the grated Parmesan. Stir, cover and leave to rest for a few minutes.

Heat a little oil in a small frying pan/skillet over medium heat. When hot, add the remaining sage leaves and cook for a few seconds only until just crisp. Drain on kitchen paper. Serve the risotto on warmed plates, with a scattering of sage leaves, and offer more grated Parmesan at the table.

pumpkin & pea risotto

WITH TOASTED PUMPKIN SEEDS

A vivid orange colour speckled with green peas, this risotto is a delight to eat and looks pretty on the table. The peas pop in your mouth, the seeds give a satisfying crunch and the spicy kick gives it a memorable flavour.

125 g/1 stick unsalted butter

3 tablespoons pumpkin seeds

¼–½ teaspoon ground chilli/chili

about 1 litre/4 cups vegetable stock or chicken stock

1 large onion, finely chopped

500 g/4 cups fresh pumpkin or butternut squash, peeled and finely diced

300 g/1½ cups risotto rice

3 tablespoons chopped fresh mint

200 g/1½ cups frozen peas, cooked and drained

75 g/¾ cup freshly grated Parmesan cheese

sea salt and freshly ground black pepper

SERVES 6

Melt half the butter in a saucepan until foaming, then add the pumpkin seeds. Stir over medium heat until the seeds begin to brown, then stir in the chilli/chili, salt and pepper. Remove from the heat and cover to keep the seeds warm.

Put the stock in a saucepan and keep at a gentle simmer. Melt the remaining butter in a large, heavy saucepan and add the onion. Cook gently for 10 minutes until soft, golden and translucent but not browned. Add the pumpkin or squash and cook, stirring constantly, over the heat for 15 minutes until it begins to soften and disintegrate. Mash the pumpkin in the pan with a potato masher. Stir in the rice to coat with the butter and mashed pumpkin. Cook for a couple of minutes to toast the grains.

Begin adding the stock, a large ladleful at a time, stirring gently until each ladle has almost been absorbed by the rice. The risotto should be kept at a bare simmer throughout cooking, so don't let the rice dry out – add more stock as necessary. Continue until the rice is tender and creamy, but the grains still firm. (This should take 15–20 minutes depending on the type of rice used.)

Taste and season well with salt and pepper and stir in the mint, peas and all the Parmesan. Cover and let rest for a couple of minutes so the risotto can relax, then serve immediately, sprinkled with the pumpkin seeds.

pies & bakes

pumpkin scones

These are scones that your guests will remember for a long time. The pumpkin purée, flavoured with maple syrup, cinnamon and vanilla, is what makes them so moist and so absolutely delicious.

300 g/2½ cups peeled pumpkin or butternut squash, chopped into 3-cm/1¼-in. pieces

40 ml/3 tablespoons pure maple syrup

2 tablespoons vanilla extract

1 teaspoon ground cinnamon

350 g/2⅔ cups gluten-free self-raising/rising flour plus 1 teaspoon baking powder OR 340 g/2½ cups plus 1 tablespoon gluten-free plain/all-purpose baking flour plus 3 teaspoons baking powder and 1 teaspoon xanthan gum

100 g/1 cup ground almonds

115 g/1 stick butter

50 g/¼ cup caster/superfine sugar

for the maple glaze

40 ml/3 tablespoons maple syrup

20 g/1 tablespoon butter

40 g/scant ¼ cup caster/superfine sugar

1 teaspoon vanilla extract

a baking sheet, greased and lined

a 7.5-cm/3-in. fluted cutter

MAKES 14

Preheat the oven to 190°C (375°F) Gas 5.

Put the pumpkin pieces on a large piece of double layer of foil. Drizzle over the maple syrup and vanilla extract and sprinkle with the cinnamon. Wrap the foil up well and transfer to a baking sheet. Bake in the preheated oven for 30–40 minutes, until the pumpkin is soft. Let cool, then purée in a food processor.

Put the flour, baking powder and ground almonds in a mixing bowl and rub in the butter with your fingertips. Add half the pumpkin purée and sugar to the flour and mix in. Gradually add the remaining purée a little at a time, until you have a soft dough. You may not need all the purée, depending on the water content of your pumpkin.

Put the dough on a floured work surface and use a rolling pin to roll out the scone dough to a thickness of 2–3 cm/¾-1¼ in. Stamp out 14 rounds using the cutter. Arrange the scones on the prepared baking sheet a small distance apart. Bake in the preheated oven for 12–15 minutes, until the scones are golden brown and sound hollow when you tap them.

To make the glaze, put the maple syrup, butter, sugar and vanilla extract in a small saucepan and gently heat until the butter has melted and the sugar dissolves. Brush the glaze over the warm scones using a pastry brush. Serve warm or cold.

These scones are best eaten on the day they are made, but can be frozen and reheated before serving.

pumpkin raisin bread

This sweet golden bread tastes beautiful plain or buttered, but if you can't get too much of a good thing, spread with strawberry conserve and cream. Lots of hot green tea or strong caffè latte are also required.

400 g/2¾ cups strong white bread flour

½ teaspoon salt

1 sachet easy-blend dried yeast*

65 g/4½ tablespoons unsalted butter

190 g/1½ cups cooked mashed pumpkin

125 ml /½ cup double/heavy cream, heated

75 g/½ cup raisins

1 egg, beaten, to glaze

a 1-kg/2-lb. loaf pan, greased

MAKES 1 LARGE LOAF

Sift the flour and salt into a large bowl, stir in the dried yeast* and rub in the butter. Add the mashed pumpkin, cream, raisins and 65 ml/¼ cup lukewarm water. Mix to form a soft but not sticky dough. If the dough is too sticky, add more flour, 1 tablespoon at a time; if it's too dry, add lukewarm water, 1 tablespoon at a time.

Turn out the dough onto a floured surface and knead thoroughly for 10 minutes until smooth and elastic. Return to the bowl and cover. Let rise at normal room temperature until doubled in size – about 1–1¼ hours.

Knock down the risen dough. Turn out onto a floured surface and knead briefly. Shape into a loaf and press neatly into the prepared pan. Cover and let rise as before until doubled in size – about 45 minutes.

Preheat the oven to 200°C (400°F) Gas 6 . Brush the risen loaf with beaten egg, then bake in the preheated oven for 25 minutes. Reduce the temperature to 180°C (350°F) Gas 4 and bake for a further 15–20 minutes or until the turned-out loaf sounds hollow when tapped underneath. Cool on a wire rack.

*Note: If using fresh yeast, crumble 15 g/½ oz. into a jug/pitcher, add the lukewarm water and stir until blended. Add to the dry ingredients at the same time as the pumpkin. Proceed as in the main recipe.

pumpkin madeleines

WITH SAGE

These sweet, dainty Madeleine cakes make a tasty accompaniment to soups and stews but can be eaten on their own as a snack. It is important to chill the Madeleine batter before cooking to get the best results. Make these in a mini Madeleine pan for bite-size canapés, if you prefer.

100 g/7 tablespoons butter, plus extra for greasing

12 sage leaves

2 eggs

20 g/1½ tablespoons caster/ superfine sugar

100 g/scant ½ cup pumpkin purée

70 g/½ cup gluten-free self-raising/rising flour OR 70 g/½ cup plus 1 tablespoon gluten-free plain/all-purpose flour, plus ¾ teaspoon baking powder and ½ teaspoon xanthan gum

50 g/⅓ cup ground almonds

sea salt and ground black pepper

a 12-hole large Madeleine pan, greased with butter

a piping bag fitted with a large round nozzle/tip

MAKES 12

Set a frying pan/skillet over a gentle heat, add the butter and heat until foamy (make sure you cook the butter over a gentle heat to ensure that it does not brown too much). Add the sage leaves and cook for a few minutes until the leaves are slightly crispy, then remove the leaves with a slotted spoon and reserve the butter. Place one sage leaf into each hole of the greased Madeleine pan, securing in place in the centre with a little butter.

For the Madeleine mixture, whisk together the eggs and sugar in a large mixing bowl until the mixture is thick and creamy. Add the pumpkin purée, flour (plus baking powder and xanthan gum, if using) and almonds and whisk in. Add the cooled, melted sage-infused butter from the frying pan and mix together well. Season with salt and pepper, then spoon the batter into the piping bag and chill in the refrigerator for 1 hour.

Preheat the oven to 180°C (350°F) Gas 4.

Pipe the mixture into the holes of the Madeleine pan, then bake in the preheated oven for 15–20 minutes, until golden brown and the Madeleines spring back to your touch.

They are best eaten warm and on the day they are made.

pumpkin loaves

These little loaves are served in their pumpkin shells, giving you a perfect combination of roasted pumpkin flesh and wholesome loaf. The bread is made with pumpkin purée so is a wonderful orange colour. They are ideal to serve with soups and casseroles.

3 small pumpkins

olive oil, for drizzling

100 g/¾ cup gluten-free self-raising/rising flour plus 2 teaspoons baking powder OR 100 g/¾ cup gluten-free plain/all-purpose flour plus 3 teaspoons baking powder and ½ teaspoon xanthan gum

100 g/⅔ cup fine cornmeal, plus extra for sprinkling

2 eggs

60 g/4 tablespoons butter, melted and cooled

300 ml/1¼ cups milk

1 teaspoon hot smoked paprika

1 tablespoon pumpkin seeds

pumpkin seed or olive oil, for drizzling

sea salt and ground black pepper

MAKES 3 SMALL LOAVES

Preheat the oven to 180°C (350°F) Gas 4.

Cut the tops off the pumpkins and discard the tops. Place the pumpkins in a roasting pan and drizzle with olive oil. Put them in the preheated oven and roast for about 30–40 minutes until the flesh is soft but the pumpkins still hold their shape. Remove from the oven and leave to cool.

When the pumpkin is cool, use a spoon to scoop the flesh and pumpkin seeds from the insides of the pumpkin to hollow out the shells. Discard the seeds (or wash and then roast them in the oven seasoned with salt and pepper for a healthy snack).

Preheat the oven again to 180°C (350°F) Gas 4.

Sift the flour and baking powder (plus xanthan gum, if using) into a large mixing bowl and add the cornmeal and 2 generous tablespoons of the cooked pumpkin flesh. Add the eggs, melted butter, milk and paprika and whisk until you have a smooth mixture. Season with salt and pepper, then divide the mixture between the hollowed out pumpkins and return to the roasting pan. Sprinkle the mixture with pumpkin seeds and drizzle with a little pumpkin seed or olive oil. Bake the pumpkin loaves in the preheated oven for 25–35 minutes until the bread is cooked through.

The loaves are best eaten on the day they are made.

for the cookie shell

300 g/10 oz. gluten-free gingernuts/gingersnaps

100 g/7 tablespoons butter, melted

for the pumpkin Chantilly

250 g/1 cup pumpkin purée

3 egg yolks and 4 egg whites

110 g/generous ½ cup caster/ superfine sugar

250 ml/1 cup milk

½ teaspoon salt

1 teaspoon vanilla bean paste

1 teaspoon ground ginger

a pinch of grated nutmeg

1 teaspoon ground cinnamon

2 tablespoons melted butter

10 g/1½ tablespoons powdered gelatine

60 ml/¼ cup warm water

for the topping

80 g/⅓ cup caster/superfine sugar

50 g/⅓ cup shelled pecans

250 ml/1 cup double/heavy cream

23-cm/9-in. round springform cake pan, greased and lined with baking parchment

silicon mat or baking sheet, greased

SERVES 10

pumpkin chiffon pie

Unlike traditional pumpkin pie, which can be quite heavy, this spectacular festive dessert is light and airy.

For the cookie shell, blitz the cookies to fine crumbs in a blender or food processor, and add the melted butter. Stir well so that all the crumbs are coated. Press the crumbs into the prepared pan using the back of a spoon so that they cover the base and come about 3 cm/1¼ in. up the sides in a thin layer.

For the pumpkin Chantilly, put the pumpkin purée in a heatproof bowl over a saucepan of simmering water and heat for 10 minutes, stirring occasionally. Add the 3 egg yolks, 50 g/¼ cup of the sugar, milk, salt, vanilla bean paste, ginger, nutmeg, cinnamon and melted butter to the bowl, and whisk together. Cook for a further 10 minutes over the saucepan, then remove from the heat.

Dissolve the powdered gelatine in the warm water, whisking well. Whisk the dissolved gelatine into the pumpkin mixture, then leave to cool. Whisk the 4 egg whites to stiff peaks and then fold in the remaining 60 g/generous ¼ cup of caster/superfine sugar a little at a time. Gently fold the egg white mixture into the pumpkin mixture, until fully incorporated. Pour into the cookie shell. Allow to set in the refrigerator overnight.

For the topping, heat the sugar in a pan over low heat, until it melts and starts to turn golden. Do not stir the sugar, but swirl the saucepan over the heat from time to time to ensure even cooking. Watch carefully as when the sugar melts it can easily burn. Spread the pecans out on the silicon mat or a greased baking sheet and swirl over the melted sugar in pretty patterns, coating the pecans. Leave to set. These are best made shortly before serving as they become sticky when exposed to the air.

To serve, carefully slide a knife around the edge of the pan to release the cake. Whip the cream to stiff peaks, and arrange it over the top of the pumpkin Chantilly, forming soft peaks. Top with the caramelized pecans, and serve immediately.

pumpkin & cinnamon filo strudel

This crumbly, heavenly filo strudel is made with creamy, sweet pumpkin and a hint of cinnamon. It is best made using large sheets of filo pastry, but if you can't find such large sheets, simply start with smaller sheets and overlap them to make the correct size.

200 g/1¾ cups pumpkin

½ teaspoon ground cinnamon

50 g/¼ cup golden caster/ superfine sugar

20 ml/1 tablespoon vegetable oil

3 large sheets of thick filo/ phyllo pastry (47 x 32 cm/ 18½ x 12½ in.)

icing/confectioners' sugar, to dust

a baking sheet, greased

MAKES 6 SLICES

Preheat the oven to 170°C (325°F) Gas 3.

Peel and deseed the pumpkin. Grate the flesh and squeeze out any excess water. Put in a bowl and mix with the cinnamon and sugar.

Take one sheet of filo/phyllo pastry, lay it on the prepared baking sheet and lightly brush with oil. Place a second sheet of pastry on top and lightly brush with oil. Repeat with the third sheet of pastry.

Spoon the pumpkin filling along one longer side of the filo/phyllo sheets, leaving a 2-cm/¾-in. gap on either side and spreading the filling about 5 cm/2 in. wide. Fold the longer side of the pastry, nearest the filling, in about 2 cm/¾ in., then roll the pastry up, tucking in the sides as you go. When the strudel is baking, the filling will soften and some juice might seep out, so tucking in the sides ensures that not too much juice is lost.

Brush the top of the strudel with a little more oil and bake in the preheated oven for 25 minutes. The strudel should be pale gold. Remove from the oven and leave to cool for 5 minutes. Dust liberally with icing/confectioners' sugar and serve warm.

pumpkin pie

A Thanksgiving dinner would be incomplete without a pumpkin pie. This tasty, spicy dessert is usually made with canned purée, but if you can't find cans, you can make your own (see Tip, below). Butternut squash also makes an ideal substitute for the pumpkin and gives a brighter colour to the filling.

400 g/14 oz. ready-made shortcrust pastry

475-g/15-oz. can pumpkin purée or 500 ml/2 cups homemade (see Tip, right)

100 g/½ cup packed soft light brown sugar

3 eggs

200 ml/¾ cup evaporated milk or double/heavy cream

120 ml/½ cup golden syrup/ light corn syrup or light molasses

a good pinch of salt

1 teaspoon ground cinnamon

½ teaspoon mixed/apple pie spice

1 teaspoon pure vanilla extract

2 tablespoons golden or spiced rum (optional)

a 20.5-cm/8-in. metal or enamel pie plate

a maple leaf pastry cutter (optional)

SERVES 4–6

Preheat the oven to 190°C (375°F) Gas 5.

Unroll and prepare the pastry following the packet instructions and then use it to line the pie plate, trimming off the excess pastry. Either crimp the edge of the pastry or use the pastry trimmings to cut leaves to decorate the edge. Prick the base all over with a fork, then line with baking parchment or kitchen foil and baking beans and bake blind for 12–15 minutes. Remove the foil and beans and return to the oven for a further 5 minutes to dry out the pastry. Leave to cool.

Reduce the oven temperature to 160°C (325°F) Gas 3.

Place all the remaining ingredients in a food processor and process until smooth. Set the cooled pie crust on a baking sheet and pour in the filling. Bake in the preheated oven for about 1 hour or until just set. If the pastry edges are beginning to brown too much before the filling is set, cover the edges with kitchen foil before returning to the oven. Remove from the oven to a wire rack and leave to cool in the pie plate. Serve warm or at room temperature, not chilled.

Tip: If you can't find cans of pumpkin or butternut squash purée, you can prepare your own. Cut 750 g/1½ lb. of unpeeled pumpkin or squash into large chunks and bake in an oven preheated to 160°C (325°F) Gas 3 for about 1 hour. Alternatively, cook the chunks of pumpkin in the microwave in a covered heatproof bowl. (Boiling it won't work as it will make the pumpkin too wet.) When cooled, scrape the flesh from the skin and purée in a food processor.

spiced pumpkin & apple pie

for the pastry

**200 g/1½ cups plain/
all-purpose flour**

**100 g/7 tablespoons unsalted
butter, chilled**

**40 g/1 cup icing/confectioners'
sugar**

1 large/extra large egg yolk

1 teaspoon grated orange zest

for the filling

**450 g/3¾ cups prepared
pumpkin, cut into chunks**

**80 g/5 tablespoons lightly
salted butter**

**100 g/½ cup light brown or
white sugar**

**2 tablespoons golden/corn
syrup or runny honey**

3 eggs, beaten

**½ teaspoon each ground
cinnamon, ground ginger
and freshly grated nutmeg**

**finely grated zest and juice
of 1 unwaxed lemon**

**1 large cooking apple, peeled,
cored and coarsely grated**

**icing/confectioners' sugar,
to dust**

**double/heavy cream, chilled,
to serve**

*a deep, 22–23-cm/9-in. diameter,
loose-bottomed metal tart pan*

SERVES 8–10

This is an interesting twist on traditional pumpkin pie. It has a lighter, slightly sharper flavour, thanks to the addition of a sour cooking apple.

To make the pastry, put the flour, butter and icing/confectioners' sugar in a food processor with a pinch of salt and whizz until the mixture resembles breadcrumbs. Add the egg yolk, orange zest and 2 tablespoons iced water and whizz again until the dough forms a ball. Turn onto a work surface and form into a smooth ball, wrap in foil and chill in the refrigerator for 1 hour.

Preheat the oven to 190°C (375°F) Gas 5. Roll out the pastry to line the tart pan. Support the sides with foil, prick the base, then bake blind in the preheated oven for 10 minutes. Remove the foil and bake again until just light brown. Remove from the oven and reduce the heat to 180°C (350°F) Gas 4.

Meanwhile, steam the pumpkin until tender. Purée it, then let it drip in a non-reactive sieve/strainer for 30 minutes or longer. You should have about 300 ml/10 fl. oz. purée. Melt the butter, sugar and syrup together, then beat into the pumpkin purée with the eggs, spices, lemon zest and juice and apple. Pour the filling into the part-baked pastry case.

Roll out any pastry trimmings to make a decorative top. Put the pie on a baking sheet and bake in the preheated oven for about 40–50 minutes until the filling is firm and cooked through (protect the pastry edges with foil if they seem to be cooking too much). Dust with icing/confectioners' sugar and serve warm, rather than hot, with chilled double/heavy cream.

sweet pumpkin, pecan & maple syrup tart

for the pastry

180 g/1⅓ cups plain/
all-purpose flour

2 tablespoons icing/
confectioners' sugar

90 g/6 tablespoons unsalted
butter, chilled

1 medium egg yolk

1–2 tablespoons freshly
squeezed lemon juice

for the filling

25 g/2 tablespoons unsalted
butter

300 g/2½ cups prepared
pumpkin or squash, grated

50 g/¼ cup light muscovado
sugar

2 tablespoons bourbon or rum

100 g/3½ oz pecan halves,
half chopped

2 medium eggs

grated zest of 1 unwaxed
lemon

150 ml/⅔ cup dark maple syrup

½ teaspoon vanilla extract

150 ml/⅔ cup double/heavy
cream

icing/confectioners' sugar,
to dust

*a deep, 22–23-cm/9-in. diameter,
loose-bottomed metal tart pan*

SERVES 8

Here the pumpkin cuts through the rich toffee of the more traditional pecan pie, making it softer and more tender, while the maple syrup adds a subtle smokiness. Use a sweet, orange-fleshed squash or pumpkin.

To make the pastry, put the flour, icing/confectioners' sugar and butter in a food processor and whizz until the mixture resembles breadcrumbs. Add the egg yolk and sufficient lemon juice, a little at a time, to make a ball of dough. Wrap in foil and chill in the refrigerator for at least 45 minutes. Roll the dough out on a floured work surface and line the tart pan. Chill for a further 30 minutes.

Preheat the oven to 190°C (375°F) Gas 5.

Support the sides of the tart with foil and bake in the preheated oven for 12 minutes. Remove the foil, press down any air bubbles in the base and bake for another 10 minutes or until pale brown. Remove from the oven and reduce the heat to 180°C (350°F) Gas 4.

Meanwhile, melt the butter in a frying pan/skillet and gently fry the squash for about 5 minutes until tender and lightly browned. Increase the heat a little, add 2 tablespoons of the muscovado sugar and cook until it caramelizes and melts around the squash. Add the bourbon and cook briskly until a sticky syrup forms, then mix in the chopped pecans. Spoon the squash mixture into the tart case and arrange the pecan halves on top.

Beat together the eggs, remaining sugar, lemon zest, maple syrup and vanilla extract, then gradually beat in the cream. Pour the mixture into the tart case. Bake in the still-hot oven for about 35–40 minutes, until puffed up and the centre retains a very slight wobble.

for the pie crust

500 g/18 oz. ready-made shortcrust pastry

plain/all-purpose flour, for dusting

for the filling

250 g/9 oz. canned pumpkin purée (such as Libby's)

½ teaspoon salt

2 teaspoons ground cinnamon

½ teaspoon vanilla bean powder or 1 teaspoon pure vanilla extract

1 teaspoon ground ginger

a pinch of freshly grated nutmeg

2 tablespoons melted butter

200 g/scant 1 cup cream cheese

140 g/scant ¾ cup caster/ superfine sugar

3 eggs

250 ml/generous 1 cup double/heavy cream

to decorate

small and large white marshmallows

23-cm/9-in. loose-bottom, round, fluted tart pan, greased

baking beans

chef's blow torch

SERVES 10

pumpkin marshmallow pie

The filling for this pie has a beautiful orange colour and is the perfect treat to serve for Thanksgiving or at Halloween. Rich and creamy, and delicately spiced, it is delicious served with a large spoonful of clotted or whipped cream.

On a flour-dusted surface, roll out the pastry thinly into a circle just larger than the size of your tart pan. Using the rolling pin to help lift it, carefully move the pastry into the pan and press it down so that it fits snugly. Trim away any excess pastry using a sharp knife, but leave some pastry hanging over the edge of the pan. This will be trimmed neatly after the tart is baked. Prick the base with a fork and chill in the refrigerator for 30 minutes.

Preheat the oven to 200°C (400°F) Gas 6.

Line the pastry with baking parchment, fill with baking beans and bake blind for about 15–20 minutes in the preheated oven, until the pastry is lightly golden brown. Once cool enough to handle, remove the beans and parchment. Trim the top of the pastry case by sliding a sharp knife along the top of the pan. Turn the oven temperature down to 180°C (350°F) Gas 4.

For the filling, whisk together the pumpkin purée, salt, cinnamon, vanilla, ginger, nutmeg, melted butter, cream cheese, sugar, eggs and cream using a mixer, until you have a smooth cream. Pour the filling into the pie crust and carefully transfer to the oven.

Bake for 50–60 minutes until the custard is just set but still has a slight wobble in the centre. Let cool.

Decorate the pie with marshmallows, then use a chef's blow torch to lightly toast the tops of the marshmallows. Serve immediately.

The pie will keep for up to 3 days stored in the refrigerator, but only put the marshmallows on just before serving.

sweet treats

260 g/2½ cups plain/
all-purpose flour

40 g/3 tablespoons granulated
sugar

½ teaspoon salt

230 g/2 sticks butter, chilled
and diced

1 large/extra large egg yolk,
beaten

1 teaspoon vanilla extract

1 egg, beaten, mixed with
30 ml/2 tablespoons milk for
egg wash

for the pumpkin filling

140 g/¾ cup canned pumpkin
purée (such as Libby's)

1 tablespoon pumpkin pie
spice*

1 large/extra large egg

¼ teaspoon salt

75 ml/⅓ cup honey

a 7.5-cm/3-in. pumpkin-shaped
cookie cutter

24 wooden ice lolly/popsicle
sticks

MAKES 24

* If you can't buy pumpkin pie
spice, make your own by
blending 1 teaspoon ground
cinnamon, ½ teaspoon ground
ginger and ¼ teaspoon each
ground nutmeg and allspice.
Any not used can be stored
in an airtight container.

pumpkin pie pops

If you want something fun and warming to serve at
your Halloween party, look no further than these cute
and tasty jack-o-lantern pie pops – they are the perfect
spooky treat!

To make the pastry, put the flour, sugar and salt in a food processor
and pulse to incorporate. Add the butter and mix on high for
10 seconds, or until the mixture resembles cornmeal. Put the egg
yolk in a bowl and pour in 60 ml/¼ cup ice-cold water. Add the
vanilla extract and mix to combine. Add the egg mixture to the
butter and flour and pulse in the food processor for 20–30 seconds,
until the mixture just starts to come together. It should be sticking
together, not crumbly. Wrap the pastry with clingfilm/plastic wrap
and chill in the refrigerator while you make the filling.

To make the filling, heat the pumpkin purée and spice in a
saucepan set over medium heat, just long enough for the spices
to become fragrant. Remove from the heat and pour into a bowl to
cool. When the filling comes to room temperature, whisk in the
egg, salt and honey and chill in the refrigerator.

Put the pastry on a floured work surface and roll out to a 3-mm/
⅛-in. thickness. Stamp out 48 pastry shapes using the cookie
cutter. Use a sharp knife to cut out scary or fun faces from 24 of
the shapes and put in the refrigerator to chill for about 30 minutes.

Preheat the oven to 180°C (350°F) Gas 4.

Take the pastry pumpkins from the refrigerator, coat with egg wash
and lay on a baking sheet 2.5 cm/1 in. apart. Put a wooden stick in
the middle of the plain pastry shapes, then add 1–2 tablespoons of
pumpkin filling. Top each with a pastry shape with a cut-out face
and seal the edges of the pies by crimping the pastry with a fork.
Brush all the pies with egg wash. Bake in the middle of the
preheated oven for 15–20 minutes, or until golden brown. Take care
when serving as the filling may still be hot.

American pumpkin cheesecake

for the base

**200 g/7 oz. digestive biscuits/
graham crackers**

**100 g/7 tablespoons butter,
melted**

for the filling

600 g/2⅔ cups cream cheese

**225 g/1 cup clotted cream (use
crème fraîche or sour cream
if not available)**

**160 ml/⅔ cup double/heavy
cream**

**100 g/½ cup caster/superfine
sugar**

**425 g/1¾ cups canned pumpkin
purée (such as Libby's)**

4 eggs

2 teaspoons ground cinnamon

**1 teaspoon mixed/apple pie
spice**

1 teaspoon vanilla bean paste

To serve

**icing/confectioners' sugar
and ground cinnamon,
for dusting**

whipped cream

*a 26-cm/10-in. round springform
cake pan, greased and lined*

SERVES 12

This cheesecake – packed with pumpkin purée and lots of fragrant spices – is a perfect alternative to a traditional pumpkin pie for a Thanksgiving dinner. You can serve it with fresh berries and extra cream if you wish. If you can't find pumpkin purée, prepare your own (see Tip, below).

Preheat the oven to 170°C (325°F) Gas 3.

To make the crumb base, crush the cookies to fine crumbs in a food processor or place them in a clean plastic bag and bash with a rolling pin. Transfer the crumbs to a mixing bowl and stir in the melted butter. Press the buttery crumbs into the base of the prepared cake pan firmly using the back of a spoon. Wrap the outside of the pan in clingfilm/plastic wrap and place in a roasting pan half full with water, ensuring that the water is not so high as to spill out. Set aside.

For the filling, whisk together the cream cheese, clotted cream, double/heavy cream, sugar, pumpkin purée, eggs, cinnamon, mixed/apple pie spice and vanilla bean paste in a blender or with an electric whisk. Pour the mixture over the crumb base and transfer the cheesecake, in its waterbath, to the preheated oven.

Bake in the preheated oven for 45–60 minutes until the cheesecake is set but still wobbles slightly in the centre. Turn the oven off and leave the cheesecake in the oven until cool. Chill in the refrigerator for at least 3 hours, then dust the top with icing/confectioners' sugar and cinnamon to serve.

Tip: To prepare your own pumpkin purée, peel and chop pumpkin or butternut squash, then wrap in foil with a little water and a drizzle of maple syrup. Roast in a moderate oven until the flesh is soft, then purée in a food processor until smooth.

spiced pumpkin mini cheesecakes

WITH NUTMEG ICING

Have fun with these for Halloween – decorated with sugarcraft sprinkles, they're sure to be a hit with children and adults alike.

for the cheesecakes

75 g/5 tablespoons butter

125 g/4½ oz. shortcake or shortbread cookies, broken into pieces

200 g/7 oz. cream cheese

100 g/3½ oz. soft curd cheese

100 g/3½ oz. canned pumpkin purée (such as Libby's)

100 g/½ cup caster/superfine sugar

2 eggs, lightly beaten

2 pinches each of ground cloves, ginger, allspice and nutmeg

orange sanding sugar, to decorate (optional)

for the nutmeg icing

50 g/¼ cup caster/superfine sugar

100 g/3½ oz. cream cheese

½ teaspoon freshly grated nutmeg

a 12-hole muffin pan, lined with paper cupcake cases

MAKES 12

Preheat the oven to 150°C (300°F) Gas 3.

First make the base for the cheesecakes. Melt the butter in a small pan and leave to cool slightly. Grind the biscuits/cookies to crumbs in a food processor. Add all but 1 tablespoon of the melted butter (reserve this for the icing/frosting) and whizz to combine. Divide between the cupcake cases and press down firmly with the back of a teaspoon.

Put the cream cheese, curd cheese, pumpkin purée, sugar, beaten eggs and spices in an electric mixer (or use a large mixing bowl and an electric whisk). Whisk until smooth and combined. Tip the mixture into a jug/pitcher, then pour it into the cupcake cases, dividing it equally.

Bake the cakes in the preheated oven for 15 minutes. Leave to cool completely – they will set as they cool.

To make the icing/frosting, whisk the ingredients together (including the reserved butter) and put a spoonful on the top of each cheesecake.

If you are not eating the cheesecakes immediately, refrigerate them, but let them come to room temperature before eating. Sprinkle with sanding sugar, if you like. They are soft-set, so they are best eaten with teaspoons.

200 ml/¾ cup milk, warm

7-g/¼-oz. package fast-action dried yeast

60 ml/¼ cup pure maple syrup

300 g/2⅓ cups plain/ all-purpose flour

160 g/1¼ cups white bread/ strong flour

½ teaspoon salt

2 eggs, beaten

60 g/4 tablespoons butter

1 teaspoon each ground cinnamon and ginger

pinch of grated nutmeg

sunflower oil

300 ml/1¼ cups double/heavy cream, whipped

for the pumpkin custard

2 tablespoons cornflour/ cornstarch

60 g/⅓ cup soft brown sugar

1 egg plus 1 egg yolk

250 ml/1 cup double/heavy cream

1 teaspoon each ground cinnamon and ginger

2 tablespoons canned pumpkin purée (such as Libby's)

for the candied pecans

120 g/⅔ cup sugar

1 teaspoon vanilla extract

100 g/⅔ cup pecans, chopped

16 squares of baking parchment

2 piping bags

MAKES 16

pumpkin doughnuts

These maple-scented doughnuts are filled with a warmly spiced pumpkin custard.

Prepare the pumpkin custard. In a mixing bowl, whisk together the cornstarch/cornflour, sugar, whole egg and egg yolk until creamy. Put the cream and spices in a saucepan and bring to the boil. Slowly pour this over the egg mixture, whisking all the time, then stir in the pumpkin purée. Return the mixture to the pan and cook for a few minutes until thickened. Pass through a sieve/strainer to remove lumps. Leave to cool and chill in the fridge until needed.

For the pecans, heat the sugar and vanilla in a saucepan with 60 ml/¼ cup water, simmering until you have a thin syrup. Add the pecans and cook until the sugar crystallizes (about 20 minutes). Stir the nuts well, remove from the heat and set aside.

Whisk together the warm milk, yeast and maple syrup in a jug/ pitcher and leave in a warm place for about 10 minutes until a thick foam has formed. Sift the flours into a mixing bowl, add the salt, eggs, softened butter and spices. Stir, then pour in the yeast mixture. Using a stand mixer fitted with a dough hook, mix on a slow speed for 2 minutes, then increase the speed and knead for 8 minutes. Lay the squares of baking parchment on a tray and dust with flour. Divide the dough into 16, roll each portion into an oblong shape and place on a square of parchment. Cover with a clean damp kitchen towel and rest for 10 minutes. Reshape the oblongs and then let rise in a warm place for 35–45 minutes, covered in lightly-greased clingfilm/plastic wrap, until doubled in size and holds an indent when pressed. Rest again, uncovered, for 10 minutes.

In a large saucepan or deep fat fryer, heat the oil to 190°C (375°F). Holding the square of parchment, transfer each doughnut one at a time. Cook in small batches for about 1½ minutes on each side. Remove using a slotted spoon and drain on paper towels. Use a knife to cut a lengthwise slit in the doughnut. Put the custard into one piping bag and the cream into the other. Pipe a swirl of each into each doughnut, then sprinkle with the candied pecans.

125 g/1 stick unsalted butter, softened

200 g/1 cup dark soft brown sugar

1 large/extra large egg

140 g/5 oz. canned pumpkin purée (such as Libby's)

340 g/2½ cups self-raising/ rising flour plus 1 teaspoon baking powder OR 340 g/ 2½ cups plain/all-purpose flour and 3 teaspoons baking powder

2 teaspoons ground cinnamon

1 teaspoon ground mixed spice

1 teaspoon ground ginger

½ teaspoon salt

250 ml/1 cup plain yogurt

for the filling

200 g/7 oz. cream cheese

125 g/1 stick unsalted butter

400 g/3 cups icing/ confectioners' sugar

for the glacé icing

200 g/1½ cups icing/ confectioners' sugar

juice of 1 small orange

orange food colouring

To decorate

3 heaped tablespoons icing/ confectioners' sugar

red and green food colouring

2 chocolate sticks

two 12-hole whoopie pie pans

MAKES 12

pumpkin whoopie pies

Decorated as cute pumpkins, these pies make a perfect Halloween treat.

Preheat the oven to 180°C (350°F) Gas 4.

To make the pies, cream together the butter and brown sugar in a mixing bowl for 2–3 minutes using an electric hand-held mixer, until light and creamy. Add the egg and pumpkin purée and mix again. Sift the flour, cinnamon, mixed spice, ginger and baking powder into the bowl and add the salt and yoghurt. Whisk until everything is incorporated. Whisk in 100 ml/½ cup hot (not boiling) water.

Put a large spoonful of mixture into each hole in the prepared pans. Leave to stand for 10 minutes then bake each pan in the preheated oven for 10–12 minutes. Remove the pies from the oven, let cool slightly, then turn out onto a wire rack to cool completely.

To make the filling, whisk together the cream cheese, softened butter and icing/confectioners' sugar. Remove 4 tablespoons of the mixture, mix in a drop of green food colouring and set aside. Spoon the remaining filling into a piping bag fitted with a star nozzle and pipe a swirl onto 12 of the pies halves. Set aside.

To make the icing, mix the icing/confectioners' sugar, orange juice and a few drops of the food colouring until it is smooth and glossy.

Cover the remaining pie halves with the icing using a round-bladed knife and leave to set. When the icing has set, mix 3 tablespoons of icing/confectioners' sugar with 1–2 teaspoons cold water and a few drops of orange and red food colouring to make a thick, darker orange icing. Spoon the icing into a piping bag fitted with a small round nozzle and pipe 5 lines from the centre of each pie. Spoon the green cream cheese filling into a clean piping bag fitted with a leaf nozzle and pipe green leaves and a curly stem on top of each pie – see right. Cut each chocolate stick into 6 pieces and put in the centre to look like stalks.

Top the cream cheese filling-topped pie halves with the decorated pie halves and your whoopie pies are ready to enjoy.

pumpkin curd tartlets

Pumpkin curd is sweeter than lemon curd and just as wonderful in tartlets. Use a dense-fleshed green or grey-skinned pumpkin for this recipe.

1 kg/8 cups pumpkin, halved, deseeded, peeled and cut into 4-cm/1½-in. chunks (to make 500 ml/17 fl. oz. purée)

5 cm/2 in. fresh ginger, peeled and grated

grated zest and juice of 1 lime

300 g/1½ cups preserving sugar

150 g/1¼ sticks unsalted butter, cut into cubes

4 eggs, beaten

for the tartlet shells

200 g/1½ cups plain/ all-purpose flour

1 teaspoon salt

¼ teaspoon sugar

100 g/7 tablespoons unsalted butter, chilled and diced

1 egg

1 tablespoon milk

icing/confectioners' sugar, for dusting (optional)

5-cm/2-in. cookie cutter

12-hole deep muffin pan, greased

MAKES ABOUT 36 TARTLETS

To make the curd, put the pumpkin in a saucepan, add 250 ml/1 cup water, bring to the boil, reduce the heat and simmer until tender. Drain, reserving the liquid. Purée the solids in a blender, adding enough liquid to make the blades run.

Squeeze the grated ginger and reserve the juice. Discard the solids. Put the lime zest and juice, ginger juice, pumpkin purée and sugar in a medium saucepan. Stir over gentle heat until the sugar dissolves. Pass through a sieve/strainer into a heatproof bowl set over a pan of barely simmering water. Add the butter and stir until melted.

Pass the eggs through a fine sieve/strainer into the bowl and stir well. Cook gently, stirring often at the beginning, then continuously at the end until the mixture coats the back of a spoon, about 30 minutes. Do not let boil or the mixture will curdle. Remove from the heat and pour into warm sterilized preserving jars. Seal and let cool. Use immediately or store in the refrigerator for up to 1 week.

To make the tartlet shells, put the flour, salt and sugar in a food processor. Pulse to mix. Add the butter and pulse until the mixture resembles fine crumbs. Put the egg and milk into a bowl and beat with a fork. Add to the food processor and pulse a few times, then process until the dough forms a ball. Wrap in clingfilm/plastic wrap and chill for 30 minutes or up to 1 week.

Preheat the oven to 190°C (375°F) Gas 5. Knead the chilled pastry briefly to soften, then roll out on a lightly floured surface. Cut into rounds using the cutter, then use to line the muffin pan. Prick the bases with a fork and cover the remaining pastry with clingfilm/ plastic wrap. Bake in the preheated oven for about 15 minutes until lightly golden. Remove from the oven, cool for a few minutes, then transfer to a wire rack. Wipe the muffin pan and repeat with the remaining pastry.

When ready to serve, fill each tartlet with a large spoon of pumpkin curd and dust with icing/confectioners' sugar, if using.

festive gingerbread bowl

for the pumpkin cream

300 g/10½ oz. canned pumpkin
  purée (such as Libby's)

½ teaspoon salt

2 teaspoons ground cinnamon

½ teaspoon vanilla bean
  powder or 1 teaspoon pure
  vanilla extract

1 teaspoon ground ginger

pinch of ground nutmeg

140 g/scant ¾ cup caster/
  superfine sugar

200 g/7 oz. crème fraîche or
  sour cream

280 g/10 oz. cream cheese

To assemble

300 ml/1¼ cups double/heavy
  cream

200 g/7 oz. treacle or ginger
  cookies

85 g/6 tablespoons butter,
  melted

300 g/10½ oz. ginger (pound)
  cake

80–100 ml/about ⅓ cup
  Armagnac

500 g/1 lb. 2 oz. ready-made
  custard sauce/crème
  Anglaise

20 small gingerbread men

trifle dish

SERVES 10

This delicious dessert is filled with rich layers of pumpkin-spiced cream and golden custard. It contains Armagnac-soaked gingerbread and treacle cookie crumbs, so omit the alcohol if you're serving it to children. For a playful feel, decorate with store-bought gingerbread men.

Put the pumpkin purée, salt, cinnamon, vanilla, ginger, nutmeg and caster/superfine sugar in a saucepan and heat for a few minutes until the purée thickens and the sugar has dissolved. Set aside until cold.

Whisk together the cooled pumpkin purée, crème fraîche or sour cream and cream cheese.

Whisk the double/heavy cream to stiff peaks. Put the treacle or ginger biscuits/cookies into a food processor or blender and blitz to fine crumbs. Stir in the melted butter so that all the crumbs are coated. Cut the ginger cake into about 18 thin slices.

Place a layer of ginger cake (about half the slices) in the base of a trifle dish and drizzle with half of the Armagnac. You can be more generous with the Armagnac if you want a really boozy dessert! Tuck some gingerbread men against the sides of the bowl.

Spoon over half of the pumpkin cream, then sprinkle with half of the buttery crumbs. Spoon over half the custard and top with the remaining ginger cake. Drizzle with the rest of the Armagnac.

Press the remaining gingerbread men around the sides of the dish and then continue to layer up the bowl with the remaining pumpkin cream and then the custard. Top with the whipped cream and sprinkle with the remaining crumbs. Chill in the refrigerator for 3 hours or overnight before serving.

pumpkin & ginger preserve

Pumpkin makes an unexpectedly fragrant and gloriously amber-coloured preserve. Serve this with scones and clotted cream, as a filling for cakes or tarts or with toast or croissants. Use any variety of pumpkin, but avoid the savoury squash such as Butternut or Red Onion. This softly set preserve will store well for at least nine months, but keep in the refrigerator once opened.

1 kg/8 cups prepared pumpkin, diced

grated zest and juice of 2 large unwaxed lemons

1 kg/5 cups granulated sugar

7.5-cm/3-in. piece of fresh ginger, sliced

500 g/1 lb. 1 oz. cooking apples, peeled, cored and chopped

50 g/1¾ oz. stem ginger in syrup, drained and cut into shreds

a small piece of muslin

kitchen string

4–5 sealable, sterilized jars

MAKES 4–5 SMALL JARS

In a large non-reactive bowl, layer the pumpkin, lemon zest and sugar. Wrap the fresh ginger and any lemon pips and flesh in a piece of muslin tied with string and bury it in the middle of the pumpkin. Pour over the lemon juice, cover with clingfilm/plastic wrap and leave in a cool place for 24 hours, stirring once.

Pour the mixture into a large preserving pan and add the apples. Tie the bag of ginger and lemon mixture to the handle of the pan so that the bag is suspended in the mixture.

Stir over low heat until the sugar completely dissolves, then increase the heat and simmer gently until the pumpkin softens. Increase the heat again and boil vigorously until setting point is reached, about 8–10 minutes*. Stir in the stem ginger. Remove the muslin bag, squeezing it against the side of the pan, then stir in the stem ginger. Let the mixture cool for 15 minutes, stir to distribute the ginger, then transfer to hot, dry sterilized jars and seal immediately.

*To test for set: As the mixture boils, it will start to become thicker and more syrupy. Take it off the heat and put a teaspoonful on a saucer that you have chilled in the refrigerator. Leave for 5 minutes, then push the surface with your finger – if it wrinkles, it has reached setting point; otherwise boil again, testing at 4–5-minute intervals.

white chocolate & pumpkin latte

A delicious, indulgent treat, this warming, spicy pumpkin drink is perfect to serve for Halloween and Thanksgiving celebrations, or simply to provide warmth – and a sweet treat – on a cold winter's day.

2 tablespoons canned pumpkin purée (such as Libby's)

100 g/3½ oz. white chocolate, chopped

500 ml/2 cups milk

a pinch of freshly grated nutmeg, plus extra to decorate

1 teaspoon ground cinnamon

½ teaspoon ground ginger

1 teaspoon pure vanilla extract

spray cream or whipped cream, for topping

blender (optional)

SERVES 2

Place the pumpkin purée and chopped white chocolate in a saucepan with the milk, nutmeg, cinnamon, ginger and vanilla. Simmer over low heat until the chocolate has melted, whisking all the time. For an extra-smooth hot chocolate, place the mixture in a blender now and blitz for a few seconds. This is optional, though, as you may prefer the drink with the slight texture of the purée.

Return the hot chocolate to the pan if necessary, and heat again, then pour into two heatproof glasses or cups. Top with cream and finish with a pinch of grated nutmeg. Serve immediately.

index

recipe credits

Acland Geddes and Pedro da Silva
Pearl barley & roast pumpkin salad
Thanksgiving roast pumpkin

Belinda Williams
Butternut squash & orange soup
Pumpkin & mushroom soup

Ben Fordham and Felipe Fuentes Cruz
Roasted pumpkin

Brian Glover
Beef stew with squash
Chicken & butternut squash tagine
Fish, pumpkin & coconut curry
Pasta with pan-fried squash & walnut
Pumpkin & ginger preserve
Pumpkin fondue
Pumpkin gnocchi
Pumpkin, pancetta & sage risotto
Roasted flat mushrooms
Roasted squash, chickpea & chorizo soup
Spiced pumpkin & apple pie
Spiced squash & feta filo pastries
Spicy pumpkin & coconut soup
Squash, goats' cheese & tomato tarts
Squash & sage frittata
Sweet pumpkin, pecan & maple syrup tart
White chocolate & pumpkin latte

Carol Hilker
Pumpkin pie pops

Dunja Gulin
Healing azuki bean & pumpkin stew
Miso pumpkin soup
Pumpkin, carrot & red lentil soup

Elsa Peterson Schepelern
Pumpkin curt tartlets
Pumpkin raisin bread
Stuffed sugar pumpkins

Fiona Beckett
Roast pumpkin & garlic polenta

Fiona Smith
Prosciutto & pumpkin terrine

Ghillie Başan
Creamy pumpkin soup
Moroccan honey-glazed pumpkin
Pumpkin, apple & sultana tagine
Roasted pumpkin wedges
Tagine of spicy roasted pumpkin wedges

Hannah Miles
American pumpkin cheesecake
Festive gingerbread bowl
Pumpkin chiffon pie
Pumpkin doughnuts
Pumpkin loaves
Pumpkin madeleines
Pumpkin marshmallow pie
Pumpkin scones
Pumpkin whoopee pies

Isidora Popović
Pumpkin & cinnamon filo strudel

Jordan Bourke
Pumpkin & coconut laksa

Kathy Kordalis
Squash, blue cheese & sage pizza

Laura Washburn
Butternut squash & sage mac & cheese
Pumpkin & rice gratin
Roasted butternut squash grilled cheese sandwich

Leah Vanderveldt
Thai pumpkin & vegetable curry

Maxine Clark
Pumpkin & pea risotto
Pumpkin pie

Nadia Arumugam
Beef with butternut squash

Ross Dobson
Orange vegetable & spring onion pilau
Pumpkin & Gorgonzola risotto
Spiced pumpkin & spelt salad
Tagliatelle with pan-fried pumpkin

Sarah Randall
Spiced pumpkin mini cheesecakes

Tori Haschka
Roast pumpkin & apple soup

picture credits

Martin Brigdale
page 40

Peter Cassidy
pages 8-16, 20, 23, 28, 31, 36, 43, 50, 61, 66, 70, 74, 78, 81, 84, 91, 95, 99, 102, 114, 118, 121

Tara Fisher
page 65

Winfried Heinze and Gloria Nicol
page 6

Richard Jung
pages 19, 77, 87, 88, 96, 124

Mowie Kay
page 24

William Lingwood
page 132

Jason Lowe
page 100

Steve Painter
pages 27, 35, 46, 49, 54, 57, 73, 92, 117, 122, 127, 128, 135, 139, 141

William Reavell
pages 2, 58, 62, 69, 105, 109-113

Debi Treloar
pages 39, 106, 136

Kate Whitaker
pages 1, 5, 32, 44, 131

Isobel Wield
page 53

Clare Winfield
page 82